Albuquerque

ALBUQUERQUE

A City at the End of the World

V. B. PRICE

Photographs by Kirk Gittings

UNIVERSITY OF NEW MEXICO PRESS ▪ ALBUQUERQUE

For Rini

Preface and Chapter Nine © 2003 by V. B. Price;
© 1992 by V. B. Price. All rights reserved.
Photographs © 1992 by Kirk Gittings. All rights reserved.
Second edition, second paperbound printing

10 09 08 07 06   2 3 4 5 6

ISBN-13: 978-0-8263-3097-0
ISBN-10: 0-8263-3097-5

LIBRARY OF CONGRESS CATALOGING-IN-PUBLICATION DATA

Price, V. B. (Vincent Barrett)
Albuquerque : a city at the end of the world / V. B. Price.— 2nd ed.
p. cm.
Originally published: A city at the end of the world. 1st ed.
Albuquerque : University of New Mexico, c1992.
ISBN 0-8263-3097-5 (pbk. : alk. paper)
1. Architecture—New Mexico—Albuquerque.
2. Albuquerque (N.M.)—Buildings, structures, etc.
I. Price, V. B. (Vincent Barrett) City at the end of the world. II. Title.
NA735..A47 P75 2003
720'.9789'61—dc21
2003005511

A shorter version of Chapter 9 appeared in the winter 2002 edition of the
University of New Mexico School of Law's *Natural Resources Journal*.

Contents

Preface to the New Edition

THE LAST CHAPTER of this second edition of *A City at the End of the World* is called "Promises, Promises," and was written almost exactly ten years after the first edition went to press. Back then, I'd produced a newspaper column at least once a week, virtually every week, for twenty years. That came out to some 1040 columns. Ten years later I've written at least 520 more, all at The *Albuquerque Tribune*. I'd say half of them have been about Albuquerque's built environment. So, you'd think I'd know something about the subject. But it truly does feel like I understand less and less all the time. Certainty gets replaced in my mind by trifling confusions, which in turn collapse into cavernous self-doubts. And I wonder how anyone could ever consider himself or herself an expert on any city or even any small town.

In ten years, though, I realize that with my uncertainty has come an increasing distaste for the spin doctoring of boomers and profiteers. I am more conservative than ever about the conservation of cultural and natural resources. And I've come to think of myself as someone longing to meet a convincing, long-term urban pragmatist—the short-term variety having come close to running us into the ground with their spendthrift myopia when it comes to land use and water. I'm not interested in sustaining the status quo either. In ten years I've become more of an environmentalist, too, opposing gas guzzling of all kinds, as well as meandering, anarchical fringe development, and anything else, for that matter, that compromises the flourishing life of our habitats and open lands. But I have to say, too, that I've become deeply suspicious of environmental political logic when it's based on ideology rather than an old-fashioned conservation ethic.

Nothing in the last ten years of confusion has changed my mind about cities reflecting the values of their citizens. Every single thing in a city that didn't grow from genes or geological processes has been consciously designed or chosen by human beings to serve some purpose or as a means to some end—everything—competently designed or not. You can't find a doorknob or a streetlight, a water filter or an asphalt patch that was made by natural selection. Everything is the product of intention, of human genius or human folly. I still think it's possible to assess the character of a city's residents, their leaders, and their politics, by the evidence of how they've inhabited the landscape they've been given and how they reflect the culture that they share. When I first started reviewing the city, in 1971 at The *New Mexico Independent,* I was appalled by how culturally wasteful I thought it was, how unresponsive most of it seemed to its climate and to its majestic natural setting, and how miserably planned it all appeared. I feel pretty much the same today, surveying our ongoing lost promise. But now I'm more in a muddle about why that's so. And all I can do is fall back on what seems to be the utterly obvious realization that while a city is a reflection of the values of its citizens, those values are generally a complete mess and jumble of class, culture, and even language and occupation. And more often than not, these value systems compete and battle one another to a standstill with major projects and connecting tissue in cities ending up, over time, being designed by default and representing no one's set of beliefs—unless a city is blessed with an innovative and politically brilliant leadership elite. Albuquerque, with all its artists, writers, and PhD's, is strong on the gifts of genius, but leadership is not among them.

Albuquerque is more and more caught in such a tangling situation. Consensus building in the last ten years has become an all but impossible chore, as national political trends have tended to polarize virtually every urban issue. And it hasn't helped any that New Mexico's been hovering around the bottom, or at rock bottom, of national economic trends as among the poorest states in the union for as long as anyone around here can remember. Still, pride of place and a deservedly elevated sense of self-respect could have overcome a lot in our town. We live in one of the most beautiful places on earth, in the midst of cultures and traditions as fascinating as any in the world. I'm as puzzled by our willingness to dilute our identity as a New Mexican city as I am by anything. It makes no sense to me. In any other circumstance, if someone squandered such vast riches, they'd be considered a fool. Yet we squander our landscape, our open space, our water, and folks slap themselves on the back for having a good year in real estate.

Still, ten years later, I continue to feel that every place, large or small, has an identity worth respecting, an authenticity that deserves to be expressed and defended against arrogant intrusions and ignorant or disrespectful growth and exploitation. The unspoken metaphor here is still, for me, that cities are like people whose spirit can be broken or whose self respect can be fought for and nourished.

My feeling is these days that Albuquerque as a unique place in the American West might be close to having its spirit broken by New Mexico's poverty, by "globalized" and corporate design fads and junk architecture, by sprawl, and by the swamping of generic—i.e., interchangeable, placeless—design solutions. My view remains that any place, along with its land and history and way of life, has the inherent right to maintain its internal continuity, to grow respectfully, to conserve itself as rigorously as irreplaceable natural resources should be saved.

Albuquerque will always be a culturally mongrel place, with all kinds of languages, worldviews, and traditions rubbing shoulders. It's that ragtag quality that makes us who we are. And the people who love it here thrive on social and cultural contradictions as much as they do on vast distances, solitude, and wide open fields of vision. Anything that homogenizes us, wrecks our open land,

and under-appreciates our people is more offensive to me than ever.

The new last chapter of this book chronicles more or less journalistically, and less lyrically, the happenings in urban form around here for the last decade. I've found it a daunting task to condense so much peculiar, wonderful, and ghastly stuff in such a short space. I hope I haven't just added to Albuquerque's general state of confusion.

As usual, I've been helped and advised by many old friends who've rubbed the fog off my glasses time and time again. Painter and scholar Rini Price, my wife and partner for thirty-three years, has edited and evaluated every one of those 520 columns this last decade. I couldn't have done anything without her. Political scientist Richard Fox and social and political analyst John J. Cordova have helped me think through countless political and decision-making conundrums. Writer, poet, and environmental thinker Mary Beath has patiently helped me better comprehend the forces at work in natural systems and how human landscapes can operate within them. Cartoonist and naturalist Jim Rini has helped me peep over the edge of my bewilderment boosted by his healing humor. Conversations with archaeologist David Stuart, author of *Anasazi America,* have encouraged me never to lose sight of common-sense political economics, or, as he puts it, the difference between power and efficiency. Landscape architect Baker Morrow's clarity about land and the people who depend on it has inspired me for more than a decade. And Em Hall, writer, water expert, and University of New Mexico law professor, helped me situate Albuquerque in the broader context of the American West when he edited an earlier version of the final chapter in University of New Mexico Law School's Natural Resources Journal. My thanks to them all.

—V.B. Price
Albuquerque, August 2002

Preface and Acknowledgments

SOMETIMES, even today, I'm surprised that I live in a place called Albuquerque—and that I call it home. For me, its name still belongs with those of other distant and exotic places like Timbuktu, Keet Seel, Shipaulovi, and Katmandu. I don't find it offensive that the *New Yorker* would run a cartoon with a line that reads "Obscure chess moves: queen's pawn to Albuquerque." I find it reassuring. I like living in a city that's the commercial capital of the most foreign state in the union. I like living in the outback, on the far frontier, in a city that everyone else thinks might as well be at the end of the world. It has its psychological advantages if you're part recluse, part romantic.

An exiled city kid from the beaches of L.A., I've lived in Albuquerque for more than thirty years, and it feels as if I always have. I count myself among those thousands of wanderers who sense they were destined to be New Mexicans. When I first crossed the Arizona/New Mexico state line in 1958, my identity with the state was immediate. The two-lane hardtop of Route 66 turned from red to black at the border, and with that transition I felt my homesickness for California replaced by a feeling of coming home. Even as a teenager I knew that I'd arrived at a promised land.[1] New Mexico was a part of me and it seemed to promise a future as optimistic as it was mysterious.

Identifying with Albuquerque, though, took a little longer. But the bond is just as deep, if oddly barbed. I came of age in Albuquerque, near the University of New Mexico, in Old Town, and around the North Valley. Rural, small-town Duke City[2] was for me an oasis in the desert between adolescence and adulthood. It was a tolerant and accepting place. It welcomed sojourners and nonconformists. It still does. But it's a hard town, too. It's made hostile by shifting cultural and political fault lines. And it often feels cold with loneliness. Many people escape to Albuquerque and, at the same time, want to escape from it. They leave their old lives behind and seek refuge in Albuquerque's isolation. But the city itself soon gets to them and they either come to hate it or find themselves looking beyond the city, to the high desert wilderness, for their solace. Albuquerque is an acquired taste. And it's only the context of its natural and human landscape that makes it worth the effort.

It was the campus of the University of New Mexico that first personalized my attachment to Albuquerque and caused me to see the city as an extension of New Mexico. In the late 1950s and early 1960s Albuquerque was still, in spirit, largely as it had been before World War II. The postwar boom didn't affect the city's character until the mid 1960s. UNM in 1958 was the most romantic environment I'd encountered since Europe. It was, to borrow Jefferson's image, a university village, but unlike any I'd heard about or seen.

Filled with Spanish Pueblo Revival–style architecture, the central campus was as uniquely New Mexican as the cultural landscape of the middle Rio Grande Valley. Here was a place in which a knowledge of the world could be gained in the sanctuary of buildings that were symbolic of the earth-connected seclusion of Pueblo villages and Hispanic mountain towns. Studying in the great reading rooms of Zimmerman Library, with their details and spaces similar to those of New Mexican adobe churches, gave me the feeling that learning was serious business, perhaps even a religious duty.

UNM, with its aesthetic attachment to New Mexico, opened my eyes to Albuquerque's essential nature. Although its urban form had disturbing similarities to that of the car culture of Los Angeles, with its endless asphalt, smog, and commercial graffiti, Albuquerque seemed fundamentally different to me, even as a teenager. It was hard to articulate, but I came to realize that its unique sense of place came from the land around it, the river running through it, and the ancient cultures that still surround it, enduring despite a normally fatal proximity with the modern world.

In the early 1960s, Albuquerque's leaders were unconcerned that its unique character was being threatened by uncontrolled growth. By the early 1970s, however, environmentalists, historic preservationists, and others interested in quality-of-life issues had risen to public prominence. Albuquerque found itself embroiled in what would prove to be a more-than-twenty-year struggle to conserve its New Mexican identity while continuing to benefit from the prosperity of its growth.

It was in 1971 that Marc and Mary Beth Acuff and Ian McLeod of the *New Mexico Independent* asked me to write a weekly column about Albuquerque. Having spent a number of years writing reviews of films, books, and operas, as well as being a police and court reporter, I called the column "City Review," and decided to review Albuquerque's architecture and urban form as one would look critically at any other creative work. I am not, however, a historian, an architect, or an urban planner. I am a poet and a journalist with university training in anthropology and literature. I wrote my column from the perspective of an inquisitive and opinionated citizen heavily influenced by his early experiences of love for New Mexico. Its tone was one of critical affection. The column evolved from purely an urban review to one dealing with a variety of aesthetic, political, and environmental issues. It has appeared in one form or another in the *New Mexico Independent, Century Magazine*, which I edited in the early 1980s, the *Albuquerque Journal*, the *Albuquerque Tribune*, *Artspace*, and *New Mexico Magazine*, which I also edited for a time.

The column has generally taken the position that cities are the creations of citizens as well as the products of economic, technical, and political forces. As the work of citizens, cities can be judged and modified by citizens. In fact, all cities are subject to constant critical evaluation by those who inhabit them. Healthy cities are those in which the critical under-tone is made public, in which citizens publicly respond to their surroundings. In the column I've held that in times of rapid change the heroes of cities are those publicly interested laypersons who inform themselves, join forces with local architectural talent, progressive business people, and plan-ning professionals, and work to manage urban growth so it benefits the city rather than overwhelms it.

• • •

As an outside observer, and an independent student of plan-ning and architecture, I've been educated by many wise friends and advisors, and have come under the influence of a number of other writers. Lewis Mumford's *The City in History* and Alvin Toffler's *Future Shock* made lasting impressions on me, as did W. Warren Wagar's study of "utopia and cos-mopolis" entitled *The City of Man*. Historian James Clifford, in his book *The Predicament of Culture*, helped me focus on the future as well as on the past. Ian McHarge's *Design with Nature* and Gregory Bateson's *Mind and Nature* cleared my head and started me thinking about the land in the same way that historian Marc Simmons's articles and histories of Albuquerque and New Mexico helped me come to grips with change.

Albuquerque is blessed with a number of gifted urban thinkers. Their intellectual generosity over the years has helped me grow from the isolation of personal taste into perhaps a wider, though still personal, point of view. Architect George Clayton Pearl has talked with me about his art and profession for nearly twenty years. Architectural historian Edna Heatherington, along with urban historian Robert Wood, Southwest archaeologist David Stuart, and curator of history at the Albuquerque Museum Byron Johnson, have treated me like a colleague and made their research and insights available to me. The intellectual generosity and creative vigor of architectural historian Chris Wilson have been an enduring boon and inspiration. Design researcher and consultant Min Kantrowitz, architect Rina Swentzell, and historic preservationists Susan Dewitt and Mary Davis have helped me find my way through many confusions and gaps in knowledge. Former Albuquerque city manager Herb Smith, the late architectural historian Bainbridge Bunting, and University of New Mexico Architect Emeritus Van Dorn Hooker have been wise guides and inspirations from the start. I could not have completed this project without the generous help of UNM librarian Carolyn Mountain, to whom I am deeply grateful. I am also indebted to environmental activists such as the late Ruth Eisenberg, Ellie Mitchell, and Joan and Hy Rosner, whose energy, optimism, and commitment have taught me that even cities can be made healthier through love.

My wife Rini Price has influenced my thinking as much as anyone. She has read and edited everything I have written on the subject for the last twenty years. Her insight and

sensitivity have opened my mind and eyes daily from the beginning. My editor and friend, UNM Press Director Beth
Hadas, has made an atmosphere of candor and support without which a book as personal and speculative as this could
not have been attempted.

It's been my great good fortune to work with photographer Kirk Gittings on this and other projects. His powers
of perception and composition have helped me realize my
own intuitions about the relationship between the natural and
the human landscapes. His portfolio of photographs in this
volume gets, I think, to the ironic essence of Albuquerque's
compelling character.

I owe special thanks to Roland Dickey, Katherine Simons,
John Cordova, Jim Rini, Richard Fox, Connie Adler, Judith
Nelson, and the late Dudley Wynn for their wisdom and
kindness over the many years I have worked on this project.

Albuquerque
1991

Photographs

BY KIRK GITTINGS

*1. Hyatt Regency Hotel from the top of the
City/County building downtown*

2. Two West Mesa volcanoes

3. From Pat Hurley Park on the West Mesa looking southeast

4. Santa Barbara cemetery, Odelia and Edith, looking southwest

5. Spillway with graffiti on Juan Tabo

6. The "Star Being," Petroglyph National Monument

7. *The reconstructed Kiva at the ruin of*
Kuaua Pueblo, Coronado State Monument

8. The Sandias from Kuaua

9. Alumni Memorial Chapel, UNM, by John Gaw Meem

10. Mary and Joseph, Santa Barbara cemetery

11. Los Duranes Chapel, new Old Town

12. San Ignacio Church, Santa Barbara-Martineztown

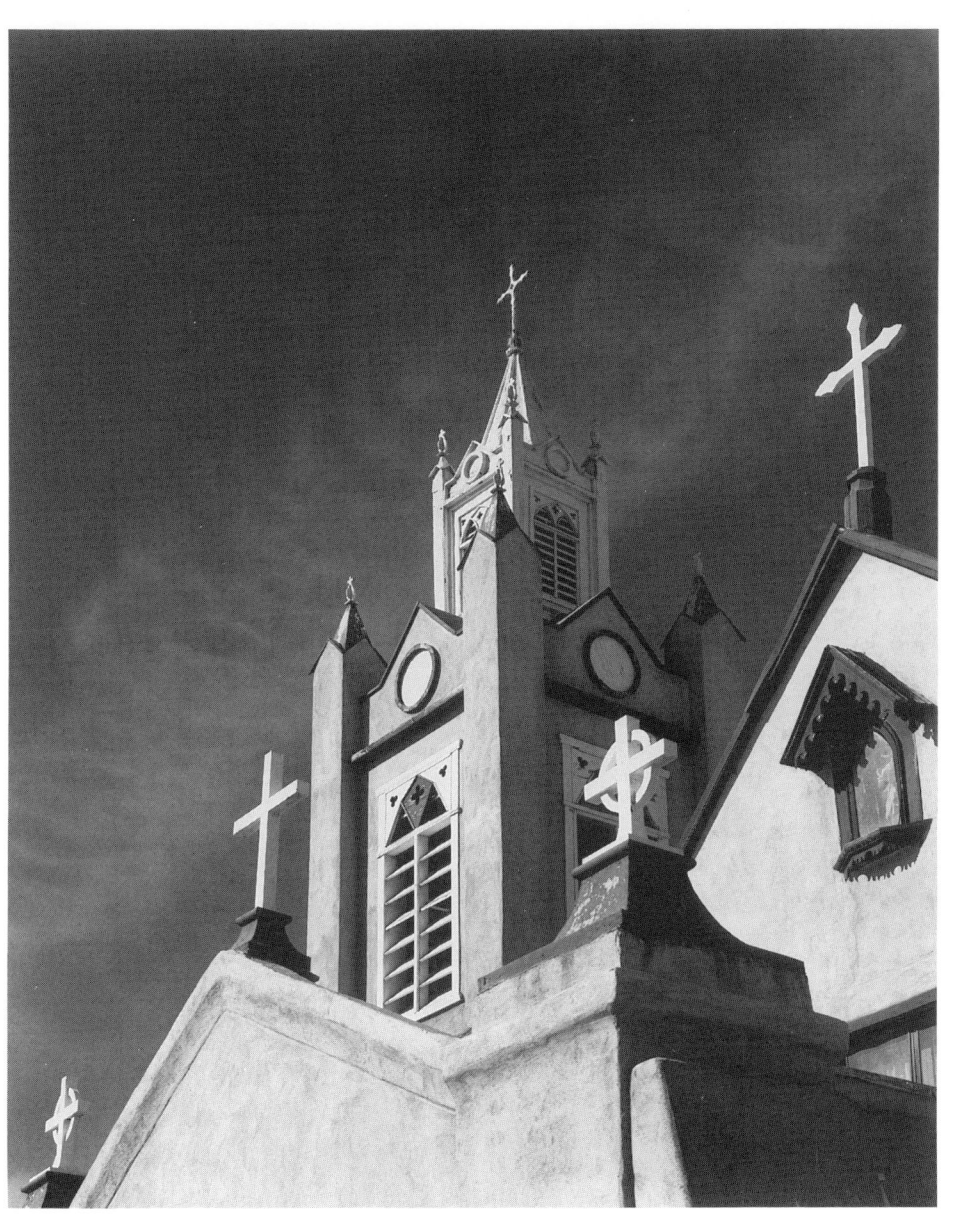

13. San Felipe de Neri, Old Town

14. *Quarai Mission Church, Salinas National Monument*

15. *The Beach Apartments by architect Antoine Predock*

16. Architect Bart Prince's personal residence

17. East Mesa water storage tank

18. A drainage ditch in the North Valley

19. The Sandias from the Rio Grande Nature Center

20. Tanoan development and golf course, looking southwest

21. Sandia Peak from the Elena Gallegos open space area

A
City
at the
End
of the
World

The Value of Locality

VARIETY means viability. In the broadest sense, that biological axiom applies as much to cities, and the cultures they nourish, as it does to the evolution of plants and animals. Just as genetic variety in the form of mutation and local variation furthers the opportunity for survival in nature, so does variety in urban habitats and cultures foster the originality and flexibility needed by humanity in its struggle to create a more healthy, beautiful, and peaceful world.

In the communications network of the twenty-first century, urban cultures will form the matrix of social and intellectual evolution. Nearly half the world's people now live in cities.[1] And though excessive urbanization is a chief factor in the global environmental crisis, the growth of cities is the dominant demographic trend of the future.[2] It is from cities, large and small, that ideas and values will emerge which could well determine the fate of both humankind and the natural environment as we know it.

Excessive urbanization in the last fifty years has brought explosive growth in major cities and has contributed to the collapse of many rural cultures and economies. Booming growth has also threatened the cultural integrity of midsized cities, such as Tucson, Memphis, Tulsa, Colorado Springs, and Amarillo. In an increasingly interdependent and homogenizing global culture, a planetary perspective is necessary for the sympathetic study of urban localities, even ones as seemingly obscure as Albuquerque, New Mexico, the thirty-sixth largest city in the nation.[3] A global point of view empowers localities with the importance they deserve as nurturers of human potential and usurps from major urban centers their self-fostered illusion of cultural and intellectual superiority. Sociologist Todd Gitlin put it handsomely when he wrote in 1989 about the "promise of a seriously global culture." It would not, he asserted, "be brought to us courtesy of McDonald's, not by the imposition of the master culture over the minor, the elite culture over the popular." Rather, the overriding principle of this global culture "has to be the preservation of the other. The hallmark is coexistence" between the global and the local.[4]

But distinct local urban cultures today are similar to endangered species. They are everywhere threatened by overpopulation, by maelstroms of competing values, by corporate culture and its symbolism, by national and international building fads that undermine the psychological potency of traditional urban patterns, and by the defacing banalities of a universal consumer culture supported by instant, worldwide communications. Cities that contribute the benefits of variety to the struggle for a better world satisfy a broad range of human needs and not just financial ones. Urban environments that are spawned by values which consider human beings to be mere consumers, or socioeconomic and political cogs, are often hostile places, subversive to the nurture of mental and spiritual health. Urban localities are like endangered species today because the economic and environmental pressures of excessive urbanization are creating cities that treat people as generic entities rather than as complicated personalities who are deeply affected by the emotional and cultural messages conveyed by their built environments.

It is in response to this ongoing compromise of urban identity and sense of place that this book is written. Its conceptual framework consists of three interlocking perceptions that honor the value of locality.

First, cities are both built environments and the natural environments in which they are built. Cities are part of a natural ecology, just as human nature and nonhuman nature are parts of a single natural order.

Second, cities constitute a socio-ecological art form that consists of design, commerce, public policy, and the specific natural and cultural conditions of the place they both inhabit and help create. Cities are artifacts of human values. As artifacts, they can be used to understand the culture and priorities of the people who give them life.

Third, every city is its own place with its own integrity. Each is more than the sum of its parts, a subjective as well as an objective phenomenon. A city's built environment—its streetscapes, infrastructure, parks, open spaces, as well as its building interiors and facades—cannot be understood by applying comparative methods and generic standards alone. The nature of each city must also be assessed in the context of its historical and structural character. Albuquerque serves as a fascinating specimen of the meaning of local identity. Modern Albuquerque is an eclectic midden, filled with the corpses of national fads and urban solutions, as well as with the remains of a turbulent and eccentric local history. Its *genius loci,* or sense of place, however, has a tenacious presence despite the ravages of rapid growth.

I have characterized Albuquerque as a city at the end of the world for two reasons: first, because of its cultural obscurity and geographic isolation from national and international power centers; and second, because of its status as the brain center of America's nuclear defense industry,[5] and probably as a first-strike target in the case of nuclear war. This paradox of obscurity and centrality gives poignancy to Albuquerque's long-time desire to be something more than an afterthought on the list of America's urban destinations.

At the beginning of the 1990s, despite spurts of rapid growth, Albuquerque remains what could be called a tributary city. It has not made the big time. It connects with mainstream America, but its sources remain in the hinterlands. Mainstream America looks upon Albuquerque as a marginal place, provincial and even primitively undeveloped.

Like other emerging towns and cities in the American West and in the developing world, Albuquerque's vulnerability to mainstream cultural backwash and population flooding puts it on the list of endangered places. And because it is geographically set in the middle of a true natural wilderness—the riverine, high desert plateau of central New Mexico—Albuquerque is particularly defenseless against the fast-paced flow of the mainstream world. The attraction of its emptiness seems as irresistible as gravity. Its image is not only that of an impoverished, charm-ridden hick town eager for tourist jobs and glitz, but its "wilderness" status makes it seem ripe for the picking, like certain portions of the Amazon basin or what used to be the deserted beaches of the Kaanapali Coast.

In this light, Albuquerque may be looked upon as an urban laboratory in which the phenomenon of cities and outbacks endangered by growth can be examined close at hand. Albuquerque's development from an isolated eighteenth-century Spanish village to a Sunbelt city of "great opportunity"[6] with more than 500,000 people serves as a metaphor for local cultures struggling to grow and at the same time maintain the nurturing stability of their sense of place.

Former Albuquerque planning director Jack Leaman observed when he left the city in 1986 that

> a quality growth program must be developed. . . . The alternative is to lose the special sense of place and the diversity of life styles which make Albuquerque different from other major growth cities. Albuquerque should not become another Phoenix, Dallas, or Denver, or look like Anywhere U.S.A.[7]

In agreeing with Leaman, I take the view in this book that New Mexico is a frontier contact zone "remote beyond compare," as conquistador Diego de Vargas described it in the seventeenth century.[8] As New Mexico's major city, Albuquerque is blessed with its own socio-ecological and spiritual identity. But it is also cursed by the conquest mentality of many of its newcomers. Albuquerque's history can be seen as a series of scrambling adaptations to the future shocks of episodic rapid growth. In coping with disruptive change, Albuquerque has managed to maintain its tenuous identity with New Mexico, I think, because those who have loved the state's eccentricity have had more influence and persistence than those who have wanted to tame it. Even in the 1970s and 1980s when the city was overwhelmed by the Sunbelt building boom, community activists created and sustained an immensely successful open-space program, a tenacious historic-preservation effort, and more than 150 neighborhood associations and protection groups.

But Jack Leaman's call for a "quality growth program" has gone unheeded. At the start of the 1990s, Albuquerque has no political consensus regarding urban sprawl, environmental pollution, energy consumption, mass transit, and the growing gulf between the rich and the poor. It remains confused about its market niche in the highly competitive world of urban economic development. And with growth still booming on its western fringes, Albuquerque, as a distinctive New Mexican city "remote beyond compare," seems more endangered than ever.

I have organized *A City at the End of the World* around the following nine themes that deal with the problem of preserving local identity:

—the negative reputation of "backwater" places and the complex character of their actual identities;

—historic preservation as both a conserver and a destroyer of vernacular culture;

—shared history, myths, and world views as the necessary context for respectful urban growth;

—the natural landscape as the bedrock of local identity;

—the spiritual dimensions of urban ecology;

—the self-defeating mixed messages of cities without a coherent self-image;

—creating culturally sustaining architectural symbols from traditional and imported cultural motifs;

—the problems of factionalism and urban planning;

—and the political challenge of building a policy consensus around land-use, cultural, and social issues that foster sustainable development, good wages, and a sense of local identity and self-respect.

The underlying assumption of this book is that urban cultures with eccentric local identities have an immense value in the homogenizing world of the approaching twenty-first century—if they maintain their individuality. Rarity creates

value, and midsized cities with character that have maintained
a respectful relationship with their natural environments will,
in all likelihood, be extremely rare and highly valued in the
urban marketplace of the future.

1

Time and Place

F R O M an overall perspective, it is the absence of love, as much as the pressures of rapid growth, that cause eccentric cities like Albuquerque to become endangered places. Disrespectful, unloving change, which is not a part of a process of continuing transformation but an abrupt disconnection with the past, destroys local character and identity. "Transformation is a part of life . . . but it has to be transformation in terms of continuing." This is how Santa Clara Pueblo architect and art historian Rina Swentzell describes the Pueblo Indian view of change. "When you leave behind the past it is detrimental not just to yourself but to the world at large. Because you leave behind respect, connectedness—which is love."[1]

Modern Albuquerque has much to learn about survival and self-respect from its Pueblo neighbors. Dr. Swentzell's articulation of the Pueblo view of the importance of continuity highlights the fundamental problem of changing cities—to create a context of shared history, myth, and world view in which cities can manage their expansion and maintain their local identities. It is a problem faced not only by booming towns and cities in the America West and the Third World, but even by bastions of wealth and tradition such as London. Prince Charles's crusade against filling London with a "jostling scrum of skyscrapers"[2] has endeared him to the British public, which resents the disrespectful changes sweeping through its capital city. In his popular 1989 BBC documentary and book *A Vision of Britain*, Prince Charles plays the role of underdog populist educator struggling to create a historical context that will help London preserve its sense of place in the face of encroaching global architectural fashions.

Developing a shared sense of history in modern Albuquerque is a formidable task as well, despite nearly a century of tourism, scholarship, and regional architecture all based on the lure of New Mexico's unique landscape and ethnic mix. The population boom since the end of World War II has flooded the city with people who do not have a romantic attachment to the state. And our schools, businesses, and elected leaders generally do not recognize the pressing need for a long-term, citywide effort at cultural and historical advocacy and education.

Albuquerque's urban history is complex but not difficult to grasp. It can be divided into three major eras: the *Anasazi/Pueblo* from ca. A.D. 1200 to the Spanish reconquest in 1692–93; the *agrarian Hispanic* from ca. 1600 to 1880 and the coming of the railroad; and the *eclectic American* from 1880 to the present.

For most of its long history, the Albuquerque area has been a slow-changing, distant, almost invisible place, wracked by wars and physical hardship, and blessed by seasons of serenity. When the Spanish arrived, the Albuquerque area was the sanctuary for Anasazi refugees from the great diaspora that followed the abandonment of Chaco Canyon and other Four Corners sites. Imagine the middle Rio Grande Valley without a modern city in the middle of it—just the sweep of the encircling mountains, the austerity of the desert, and the Eden of the bottomlands surrounding the unpredictable river with sculptural patterns of carefully tilled fields, earthen home-steads, and adobe villages. During the Hispanic period this was, indeed, the very end of the Spanish Colonial world. A tiny number of priests, soldiers, and farmers inhabited the re-gion, isolated in the visionary solitude of the land, contending with sporadic raids from nomadic peoples—raids that really didn't end until 1865 when Kit Carson conquered the Nava-jos. This agrarian, almost geologic pace of life was radically disrupted with the coming of the railroad and the Ameri-canization of the valley. Mirroring and magnifying the first influx of European culture from 1540 to 1598, the railroad brought with it a rush of newness, a revolutionary alteration in the rate of change, a "future shock" that has hit the valley in shock wave after shock wave ever since.

Albuquerque's growth in the wilderness can be usefully ex-plored by focusing on a number of historical turning points and by following the tracks of its urban expansion.

Somewhere in the vicinity of the year A.D. 1200, the year that Cambridge University was founded and Paris began de-veloping into a capital city, Anasazi refugees from the urban centers of the Four Corners area and the Mogollon Moun-tains began moving into the middle Rio Grande Valley, re-placing or perhaps incorporating indigenous Tiwa-speaking Pueblo people who had displaced the Basketmakers some three hundred years before. By 1300, the Anasazi population had grown to perhaps fifteen thousand people living in as many as forty multistory stone and adobe cities between what is now the modern town of Bernalillo and Isleta Pueblo.[3] The Spanish called this region the Province of Tiguex. It is based on this ancient urban tradition that Albuquerque can make its claim to being the longest continually inhabited major urban area in North America.

A City at the End of the World

In 1598, the Spanish moved into what is now New Mexico, not only as explorers but as settlers and missionaries. Although native peoples had been disrupted when the Spanish first explored the area some sixty years before, the arrival of Juan de Oñate and his followers signaled the first permanent infusion of European civilization north of Mexico.

After more than eighty years of religious and political persecution, a confederation of Pueblos revolted against the Spanish in 1680. Part of what the Mexicans called the Great Northern Uprising, the Pueblo revolt was the only successful Native American rebellion in the history of New Spain, or, for that matter, the North American continent. The significance of the Pueblo Revolt for the culture of modern Albuquerque is that it effectively preserved the way of life of an indigenous, pre-Columbian people, permitting them to retain their cultural integrity despite their proximity to the normally rapacious European milieu. No other city in North America and few cities in the world are privileged to have as their neighbors tribal people who can trace their urban roots back more than a thousand years. When the Spanish reconquered New Mexico in 1692–93, the Pueblos adopted a two-culture strategy for survival, living a modified European existence on the surface, while nurturing and perpetuating their native culture in private.[4] This strategy has served them well for nearly three hundred years and has allowed them to withstand social pressure from not only the early Spanish, but also the Mexicans, the frontier mercantile Americans, the population explosion of the cold war era, and the contemporary culture of commerce.

The year that Benjamin Franklin was born in Boston, the Villa de Albuquerque was established by the Viceroyalty of New Spain near the Bosque Grande de San Xavier on the banks of the Rio Grande, west of the farming settlement of

Atrisco at what today is known as Old Town.[5] It was 1706—
the year German composer Johann Pachelbel was born and
Henry Mill in England built the first carriage springs. In
northern Europe, the Enlightenment was dawning, but in the
far reaches of the northern frontier of New Spain the light
of progress was still largely spiritual and otherworldly, en-
nobling the hardship of pioneering country life and fortifying
the soul against natural disasters and the pains of an endless
Indian war.

In 1821, Mexico gained its independence from Spain and
ended the Spanish Empire's policy of isolation in its northern frontier, opening New Mexico to American traders who
would soon establish the Santa Fe Trail. By 1846, when U.S.
General Stephen Watts Kearny claimed New Mexico as an
American territory in the war with Mexico, Anglo–American
trade goods and culture had already begun to influence urban
life around Albuquerque and Santa Fe. Though still a tiny
farming community centered around Old Town Plaza, Albuquerque experienced its first growth boom as it became an
outpost for the U.S. military. By 1860, Albuquerque's population had reached 1,760[6] and Midwestern merchants with
shops on the plaza had served customers for almost a decade. In 1865, after New Mexico's brief involvement in the
Civil War, conflicts with nomadic tribes, which had harassed
Europeans and Pueblo peoples in the valley since the reconquest, were effectively brought to an end with the defeat and
relocation of the Navajos.

The year 1880 marks the beginning of the modern era in
Albuquerque with the arrival of the Atlantic and Pacific Railroad. With the tracks more than a mile and a half away from
the plaza, the center of life shifted from the adobe buildings of Old Town to the iron, wood, and brick structures of

what came to be called New Town, a predominately Anglo-American, Midwestern-looking cityscape.[7] Albuquerque suddenly became a railroad town, connected to the major centers of the East. It was a technological transformation of the greatest magnitude, and permitted the city to become an important agricultural, livestock, and commercial distribution center. Two years after the railroad arrived, the area's population was estimated at twelve thousand, with seven thousand of those residing in New Town.[8]

Albuquerque might have remained little more than a frontier boomtown had it not been for the establishment of the University of New Mexico on the sand hills a mile and a half east of New Town in 1889. UNM's influence on the city, while not as direct and obvious as that of the railroad's, has been just as profound. The university gave Albuquerque an intellectual life, attracted scholars from around the world, and generally transformed a city at the end of the world into a creative frontier—a place hospitable to artists, musicians, writers, and thinkers, a hideout for those wishing to pursue the life of the mind.

From 1906 to 1909, UNM itself was the focus of a transformation. Through the visionary imagination of UNM President William Tight and architect E. B. Cristy, the UNM campus became a symbol of New Mexico regionalism. Tight and Cristy, along with designer Mary Colter, originated what came to be called the Pueblo Revival style, designing dormitories and other structures in the form of buildings found at Hopi, Acoma, and Zuni pueblos. In 1908, Tight and Cristy remodeled the Romanesque brick Hodgin Hall in the Pueblo Revival style, thereby asserting the cultural importance of indigenous forms and traditions. While New Town filled up with the monuments and fads of a conquering Anglo-

American commercial life-style, UNM took a leading role in creating a sensitivity to the cultural richness and diversity of the state.

A moment of great symbolic importance to Albuquerque's urban environment was the city commission campaign of 1916. That year, Clyde Tingley was elected alderman.[9] For the next thirty-eight years, Tingley exerted his liberal, folksy, environmentally sensitive influence on Albuquerque as the city's long-time ex officio mayor and as a two-term governor. Under Tingley's benign bossism, which lasted seventeen years longer than Richard Daley's reign in Chicago, Albuquerque began to take itself seriously as a unique American city. Tingley was influential in fostering the construction of numerous important Spanish Pueblo Revival–style buildings, many parks and public recreation areas, and an ongoing city beautification campaign, which included a sign-control ordinance and tree planting on major streets. Tingley is also responsible for the city's forest of Siberian elms, which he gave away by the thousands. Under Clyde Tingley's influence, the 1930s saw massive sums of New Deal money flow into the state, which funded major buildings at UNM, a puebloesque airport, the distinctive state fairgrounds, the zoo, the Albuquerque Little Theater, and an acceleration of flood-control work by the Middle Rio Grande Conservancy District. When Tingley lost power in the elections of 1954, Albuquerque was emerging from a period of progressive romanticism into a harsher world dominated by rapid growth and corporate, rather than local, commerce.

A decade earlier, Albuquerque began to feel the force of another turning point in the history of its cityscape when in 1945 the military-industrial complex established itself in earnest at Sandia Base, in the far Southeast Heights near the Manzano Mountains. It had been almost one hundred years since the U.S. military caused American Albuquerque's first period of booming growth in 1846. The new military presence had the same effect, but the scale was vastly different. No longer a frontier outpost, though still a Shangri-la, Albuquerque became the capital of America's nuclear war machine, the dominant site of weapons research, management, and testing. In the 1980s, Albuquerque also became headquarters for Star Wars laser research. Kirtland Air Force Base, where Sandia Labs and the Department of Energy have their offices, is New Mexico's largest concentration of employment, with some 38,600 jobs in the mid 1980s.[10] The military's presence, from 1945 onward, stimulated an already-existing tendency toward rapid eastward growth.

Partly in response to the boomtown conditions fostered by the military, Albuquerque hired its first planning director in 1950.[11] The decade of the 1940s had seen the town's population more than double in size. Land speculators and developers were determining the city's urban form. By 1951, Albuquerque had already surged northeastward to Wyoming and Menaul, with the opening of Hoffmantown Shopping Center. The city's first shopping center, Nob Hill, some three miles southwest at Central and Carlisle, had opened on the virtual edge of town only four years earlier, in response to residential development around Kirtland Air Force Base. Parts of Albuquerque had become like Los Angeles, scarred by commercial strips and filled with American Dream suburbs. The 1950s saw the full Americanization of Albuquerque, with the establishment of a zoning code in 1953, the completion of the city's first International style skyscraper, the Simms Building downtown, in 1954, and the first modern demolition of a major historic building, Castle Huning on West Central, in 1955.

During the early 1960s, Albuquerque's urban form, as we

know it today, took shape. The West Mesa began its phenomenal growth with the opening of both Rio Rancho and Paradise Hills subdivisions. Interstates 25 and 40 were completed through the city, linking the West Mesa with the Northeast Heights. Winrock Center, the state's first enclosed shopping mall, opened and, with the help of the freeways, moved the center of town once and for all out of the downtown/Old Town/UNM area.

It could be said that Albuquerque's modern political history began a decade later in 1969–70 with the demolition of the city's most famous historic building, the Alvarado Hotel, which since 1902 had symbolized Albuquerque to countless thousands of railroad travelers. The destruction of the Alvarado, coupled with the national environmental and historic preservation movements, divided Albuquerque into two political factions—one that tended to support a policy of suburbanization and urban sprawl identified with growth since the end of World War II, and another that favored controlled growth, historic preservation, downtown rehabilitation, and conservation of the natural environment. These two factions came to loggerheads in the early 1970s and committed to full combat in 1974 when environmental planner and former city manager Herb Smith lost his campaign for mayor to Republican old-guard growth proponent Harry Kinney—an engineer at Sandia Laboratories. Three years later the two factions struggled again; this time the environmental side won the mayor's race when Kinney was defeated by Democrat David Rusk.

Since 1960, with the commissioning of a federally funded comprehensive plan, a classic political dichotomy had been evolving in Albuquerque. Though municipal elections had been nonpartisan for years, the split was clearly along Democratic and Republican lines. Democrats since Clyde Tingley have tended to be more interested in fostering local business and maintaining Albuquerque's New Mexican sense of place, while engineering pragmatists have attracted Republican votes with promises of importing national corporations and establishing policies that cater to both local and out-of-town developers.

An unlikely compromise was forged between the two outlooks with the completion of the Comprehensive Plan in 1975. Disliked and mistrusted by development interests, the plan was aimed at maintaining the diversity of environments and life-styles that gave Albuquerque its special character. It even advocated the public acquisition of open space, a remarkable provision in an entrepreneurial town grown modestly rich on land speculation. The plan, which governs land use in the city to this day, was passed by a city council of mixed philosophy and signed into law by Republican Mayor Harry Kinney. It embodies as real a public consensus as Albuquerque can muster when it comes to questions of urban growth. More important than even the city charter, the Comprehensive Plan is the Magna Carta in a town in which land-use issues are the bedrock of public activism.

Turning points in urban history become more difficult to identify as we approach the present. In the 1980s, at least four events have had major significance. In 1982–83, the Rio Grande and its bosque and riparian environment were publicly recognized as invaluable urban resources after years of being ignored and trashed. The Rio Grande Nature Center opened in 1982, and a year later the creation of the Rio Grande State Park protected some 6,000 acres of river environment from Corrales to Isleta Pueblo. In 1987, events south and west of the river made it probable that the river would become the actual center of the metropolitan area, if not of the city itself. That year, a cartel of developers, owning most of the open desert west of the Rio Grande to the Rio Puerco, hyped the creation of massive planned communities that would virtually double the size of greater Albuquerque. Problems with water rights, annexation, and infrastructure remained to be worked out. In early 1990, some seventy-five hundred acres of the West Mesa escarpment, long an object of bitter land-use disputes, were designated as the Petroglyph National Monument. Activists had struggled for much of the decade to preserve the more than 15,000 examples of Anasazi rock art on the seventeen-mile-long escarpment. And also in late 1990, activists in the unincorporated South Valley, another rural region the size of the existing city, rose against provisions in an areawide planning document that mandated what they considered to be culturally and ecologically destructive transportation routes and inadequate open-space policies. Voices were heard calling for incorporation of the whole South Valley, which would leave Albuquerque with the ominous precedent of a major nontaxpaying suburb that had revolted against the influence of both city and county governments. Politicians and planners worried that a South Valley incorporation would kill all possibilities for a single metropolitan planning authority and lead to a proliferation of even more political jurisdictions, such as Rio Rancho on the West Mesa.

The secret to understanding Albuquerque's built environment today is found in its pattern of growth since 1880, when a migration of merchant- and laboring-class adventurers and urban pioneers diffused American culture throughout the middle Rio Grande Valley in less than a generation.

Between the 1890s and the mid 1920s, Albuquerque's rural and Hispanic base was further Americanized by the appearance of an intellectual elite at the University of New Mexico on the sand hills east of New Town. Americanization tended to move east and north. With the arrival of health seekers around 1900, Albuquerque began its forty years as a national health haven, a city of sanitoria for victims of tuberculosis. Some of the state's most dynamic leaders appeared on the scene during those years—including T. B. sufferers Senator Clinton P. Anderson, architects John Gaw Meem and E. B. Cristy, and physician William Randolph Lovelace.[12] Today's hospital neighborhood, on either side of I-25 and Central, is the descendant of the city's early precinct of convalescents.

From the mid 1920s to the early 1930s, when the automobile began to dominate the city and Central Avenue became part of the national highway system, Albuquerque was an exotic tourist destination. Central Avenue merchants and property owners, finding themselves on a segment of Route 66, turned main street into a tourist oasis, dotted with cowboy-and-Indian-theme motels, diners, and last-stop-before-the-desert service stations. Albuquerque flourished under the influence of a Southwest advertising myth which "industrialized" the tourist trade, creating not only a bullish market for trinket salesmen and Indian artists, but also an economically useful cartoon of Indian life and desert culture. Southwest tourist mythology, coupled with regionalist architecture and scholarship, helped Albuquerque resist the complete Americanization of its urban environment.

By the early 1940s, Albuquerque was a confusing, if heartwarming, jumble of incongruities. It was a small, All-American city with a bustling downtown that had escaped the worst ravages of the Depression. It was also the unnamed site of Wilfred McCormick's sentimental Bronc Barnett teen sports novels, and a Southwestern college town with a startling puebloid campus. It was a rough-and-tumble cow town and regional shopping center that served ranchers, farmers, miners, and reservation Indians. It was a major stop on Route 66, but

was still considered a remote health spa known for its tran-
quillity and therapeutic air and an off-the-beaten-trail tourist
find that everyone wanted to keep a secret. The city was the
commercial capital of one of North America's few centers
of indigenous Hispanic culture in a state governed largely
by bilingual Hispanic politicians. And it was a growing, Los
Angeles–like suburban car town, with handsome neighborhoods of Ranch-, Mission-, pseudo-Pueblo-, and Bungalow-
style houses spreading east as far as Carlisle, and then some.

Albuquerque's urban growth turned into a nightmare of
snarled traffic and inadequate roads by the late 1940s. It began
to follow the pattern of suburban decentralization that was
sweeping the country, especially the West.[13] In a mere seventy
years since the coming of the railroad, Albuquerque's built
environment had undergone a metamorphosis from dignified
eccentricity to burgeoning conformity. With postwar social
values, bomb research, and a pre-Sunbelt migration moving
west, suddenly America was catching up with Albuquerque
faster than ever before.

From the 1950s through the 1980s, Albuquerque has been
shaped by the policies of technocrats and engineers, many
of whom have worked at Sandia Labs in weapons research.
Supported by federal housing programs, highway funds, and
defense contracts, Albuquerque city government has taken
a hard-science, military approach to planning, which has
cleared the way for new suburbs and commercial strips.
It's been a time of boosters, fast-pitch paradise salesmen,
prosperity preachers, and subdivisions built in arroyos. City
leadership has seen its job as bulldozing the countryside to
make clear fields for incoming troops of home buyers. As
with cities all over the West, Albuquerque is losing its historic
identity and sense of place. But Albuquerque has more to lose
than most.

A City at the End of the World

Since the 1960s, Albuquerque's pattern of growth, east to the mountains and west to the volcanoes, has been dominated by the myth of the Heights and the Valley. The North and South valleys have come to be seen as sanctuaries of artists, nature lovers, Anglo and Hispanic iconoclasts and solitaries who were attracted to what remains of rural, culturally exotic, prerailroad Albuquerque and to the neighborly, Southwestern college town the city had become before and just after the Depression. The heights and mesas, the political myth has it, are filled with people who'd just as soon be living in Anaheim or Phoenix. Two kinds of people have been struggling for dominance in the urban landscape—those who are in Albuquerque out of choice and love, and who want to live amid the incongruities of New Mexico, and those who are at home in generic America, anywhere it happens to be. Such mythic dichotomies don't do justice to the nuances of a place, but they do give guideposts to the spirit of the times.

Albuquerque Journal columnist Tom Harmon, author of a wonderful Saturday column in the 1980s called "Ditch Bank Chronicles," described the post-1960s as being Albuquerque's Asphalt Period.[14] And, indeed, it sometimes seems as if the whole city has been turned into a parking lot or a shopping mall. Land-use battles have been fought between those who believe in inevitable growth—who see Albuquerque as a place to sell, a huge fortune in empty land with no strings attached—and those who believe in growth management—developers as well as urban activists—and the beneficial effect planning can have on the natural and historic environment, as well as on the general economic climate.

And, of course, the battles still rage on. Despite its comprehensive plan, Albuquerque, like most modern American urban environments, has suffered from urban sprawl. Development has gobbled up the rural countryside and threatens to splurge west into the badlands between the West Mesa and Laguna Pueblo. In the 1980s Albuquerque became a "poly-nucleated city" with no central core, despite two decades of downtown renovation. It is now dotted with "exurbs," "outtowns," "slubs," and "burbs," and is becoming, in many ways, a "nonplace urban field."[15]

The decade of the 1990s might turn out to be another major turning point. Albuquerque could continue to grow at a postwar pace, trashing its natural environment, leaving its past behind, and becoming once and for all a place-that-used-to-be—a generic place with its New Mexican essence all but erased. It's not impossible, however, to foresee a combination of environmental limitations and economic uncertainty slowing down the pace of change and giving Albuquerque time to reconsider its future and perhaps move again toward the Pueblo virtues of respect and connectedness. Such a scenario does not imply an end to growth. It does foresee, however, a political climate in which Albuquerque can make conscious choices about what kind of growth it wants. The great leaders of Albuquerque's past—Clyde Tingley and William George Tight, in particular—presided over periods of expansion but did not let growth undermine the New Mexican character of the city. While they welcomed the vitality of urban and academic immigrants, they also worked to incorporate Albuquerque's distinctive cultural and environmental identity into its patterns of development.

2

Reputation and Identity

MODERN Albuquerque finds itself in a classic double bind. It suffers from both a crisis of identity and a crisis of reputation. Its citizens and leaders don't know if they want it to be an American city, virtually interchangeable with dozens of other Sunbelt boomtowns, or a New Mexican city true to its climate, landscape, and local culture. And as a result of this confusion, the outside world isn't sure if Albuquerque is a cartoonist's gold mine, an incongruous wide spot in the road, or a big-city cousin of Santa Fe and Taos.

It wasn't always this way. When I came to Albuquerque in the late 1950s, one of the first things I noticed was that most people I met were fiercely proud of being New Mexicans, native or otherwise, and utterly delighted not to be living anywhere else. They had been enthralled by the myth of New Mexico. To them the Land of Enchantment was not a tourist slogan, but a personal reality. Most of them lived in Albuquerque out of choice. But rapid growth has made the people who hold such sentiments no longer a determining majority.

With population pressures mounting, other eccentric cities and marginal localities around the West—such as Tucson, Boulder, Amarillo, and Colorado Springs—will be faced with a double bind similar to Albuquerque's. Overwhelmed by rapid growth, their own residents won't be able to make much sense of them. These towns are becoming disquieting and confusing places. And their competitive standing in the marketplace of cities, where economic developers use urban imagery to attract corporate consumers, will suffer from comparisons with cities that have clearer, less ambivalent identities.

In Albuquerque, rapid growth—some 13 percent between 1980 and 1986 alone[1]—has changed the city's public image and urban form so radically that long-time residents tend to get disoriented in the newer parts of town. For new residents who expect a New Mexican city, modern Albuquerque can be a bewildering disappointment. While the vastness of the New Mexican landscape still dwarfs the city itself, Albuquerque's "material shell"[2]—its seedy montage of commercial strips, franchise architecture, and fast-buck developments—camouflages its Southwestern character so well that it's often impossible to find. And for new residents who expect Albuquerque to be a "mainstream city," the place can seem depressingly like a third-world resort town overrun by developers.

Albuquerque has always been more suburban, and seemingly less romantic, than the stylish and sometimes mysterious glamour towns of Santa Fe and Taos. Still, many people who choose to stay in Albuquerque do so because of their devotion to the myth of New Mexico. But, unfortunately, the world at large is oblivious to Albuquerque's mythic virtues. And the city's repellent and enigmatic exterior continues to attract a lot of bad press.

In an April 1988 issue of *Time* magazine, for instance, the war-torn West Bank of the Jordan River outside Jerusalem, with its defensive modular housing, was described with mean hyperbole as looking "eerily like the outskirts of Albuquerque."[3] Even with its noxious sprawl, the outskirts of Albuquerque look nothing like the West Bank. The city's edges still end in desert and mountain terrain with some of the world's most beautiful geological features. The place is not an urban war zone. Albuquerque's reputation hasn't been helped much either by Tom Wolfe's 1979 book on the American space program, *The Right Stuff*, in which he describes Albuquerque as a "dirty red sod-hut tortilla highway desert city that was remarkably short on charm, despite the Mexican touch here and there."[4] And to make matters worse, a 1988 study published in *Psychology Today* magazine found Albuquerque to be "in the bottom one-fourth of American cities in terms of psychological well-being" based on crime, suicide, alcoholism and divorce rates.[5] In the minds of some writers and many Americans, Albuquerque has become a metaphor for benighted places, not only a sociological badlands, but also an aesthetic purgatory of hayseeds and other rustics that might as well be called "Albujerky" as anything else.

Most galling of all, though, is that the richness and ragtag complexity of Albuquerque's urban identity is not only overlooked in the opinions of outsiders, but also by its own image makers. It seems incredible that an almost four-hundred-year-old city in one of the world's most spectacular natural settings, surrounded by the enduring spiritualism of Pueblo Indian culture and rooted in the center of an ancient Hispanic heartland, would have so much trouble creating an understandable image for itself—an image that both welcomes new infusions of wealth and brain power, and guides quality development. But local image makers have strained their imaginations to no avail. They can't deal with the city's complicated identity. The designers of a 1989 campaign by the Convention and Visitor's Bureau, for instance, thought Albuquerque had so little to recommend it that they resorted to putting up billboards with a suggestive, hand-scrawled message that read "for a good time call," followed by the bureau's phone number. No one thought it in bad taste to equate the city with a brothel.

On the other hand, Albuquerque is so desperate to heal its blighted reputation with outlanders that a 1987 television spot, circulated in East Coast markets, tried not to show any scenes with dirt in them.[6] The theme of the spot was contained in the well-crafted tag line: "Albuquerque—a little west of Washington, a little east of L.A." But the rest of the advertisement was designed to erase Albuquerque's image as a "south-of-the-border town with bad water, jackalopes, and cactus." The ad showed lots of lawns, big buildings, basketball footage, and "elegant restaurants," and left out any reference to the city's Hispanic, Indian, and cowboy heritage.[7]

Like a contrary person whose appearance is out of sync with his soul, Albuquerque's reputation either demeans its realities or replaces them with false fronts and silly frauds. The competing myths of its reputation have the city being at one and the same time a polyester junk town with low standards and lower expectations, a yuppie hot spot in the Sunbelt, and an exotic nuevo "Gringolandia"[8] that tourists and conventioneers will one day die to flock to. And so confusion reigns. No matter what civic leaders tried to do, tourists in the mid 1980s weren't coming to the Duke City in Gold Rush numbers. And new businesses weren't either. They simply couldn't see past the schlock facade of the city's "material shell." Albuquerque hasn't been a town for tourists since the growth boom at the end of World War II. Uncontrolled growth and tourism just don't mix. Of course, people who identify with Albuquerque, and love it, try to look past the inaccuracy of its various reputations and focus on their feelings for the New Mexican spirit of the place.

But New Mexico-ismo is an elusive quality. Aldous Huxley, for instance, in *Brave New World*, designated New Mexico as the "savage reservation," a place filled with outcasts who did not fit into the genetically engineered, drug-pacified society of the future. New Mexico has always been at the end of the world. And if many of Albuquerque's new residents fail to comprehend its nature, it's understandable that outlanders miss it entirely. John Naisbitt, author of *Megatrends*, for instance, completely missed the New Mexico factor in his superficial designation of Albuquerque as one of America's "ten new cities of great opportunity."[9] He treated Albuquerque as if it were just another Sunbelt city, not the unpredictable and difficult town it can often be. Albuquerque, to be sure, is a place of great opportunity, but of an aesthetic and intellectual sort. It is not necessarily one of the shiny new financial touchstones of the American West. The city cannot escape its New Mexican context. The native-born former governor of New Mexico, Toney Anaya, has called it a "third world state," and once referred to it as a "banana republic." Because of Albuquerque's similar status as a "developing" city, it has always been ripe for exploitation and colonization, but it's also been tough on fast movers and shakers. It resists change, breaks confidence, and then suddenly leaps ahead. It's a hard place to get things done, as the ambitious and powerful and civic minded have often learned.[10]

If John Naisbitt missed New Mexico, it should be no surprise either that mainstream East Coast architectural writer Robert A. M. Stern would fail to make any mention of the state in his popular 1986 book and television series *Pride of Place: Building the American Dream*. Although New Mexico is home of the nation's oldest architectural tradition, the Anasazi, and its most vital regional style, the Spanish Pueblo Revival, its pride of place slipped right past Mr. Stern's oldworld, big-city blinders. Not a word was said even about fashionable Santa Fe, not to mention Taos or Acoma pueblos, or the campus of the University of New Mexico, arguably America's most original college environment. As the state's official magazine, *New Mexico*, proclaims in its popular humor column "One of Our Fifty Is Missing," for Mr. Stern, as well as for much of the nation, New Mexico simply doesn't exist. And Albuquerque, of course, is the Gotham of that national nevernever land.

What does it mean to a nation's identity when a cultural and architectural tradition as rich as New Mexico's has been treated as if it has no value? For one thing, it means that national culture is unable to incorporate into itself the full diversity of its marginal localities and subcultures. In an age of "planetization"[11] and the transformation of the global village into a transnational metropolis, the reflex to omit what is eccentric rather than integrate it, and be enriched by it, is an ominous sign.

At the turn of the last century, American architect Louis Sullivan maintained that the relationship between culture and its artifacts is not only formative, but determining. "As you are, so are your buildings. And, as your buildings, so are you," was his proverbial way of putting it. Echoing Sullivan almost a century later, Albuquerque architect George Clayton Pearl told me that "architecture, no matter what you try to do, will be a perfect expression of the society that was." When built environments begin to lose their local identities, or when national culture can no longer identify with its distinctive parts, the relationship between creative personalities and sense of place falls apart, and serious cultural impairment is bound to ensue.

If Albuquerque is missing in the minds of most Americans, it is partly because it is easier for people to focus on less confusing places. Its cultural complexity, foreignness, and isolation make it difficult to define in a world that's used to fifteen-second sound bites and advertising clichés. In much the same way that urbanologists speak of a "crisis in language"[12] in trying to describe multicultural "decentered urban fields,"[13] such as Los Angeles, there are no handy metaphors to describe a place like Albuquerque. Yet this New Mexican crossroads seems to be a model, of sorts, for the midsized "global village" city of the future. Such cities will retain some remnants of their original conditions, but they will be on their way to becoming what Lewis Mumford would call "implosive" human environments,[14] cities in which diverse ethnic and intellectual cultures mix in highly charged and productive ways. They will be, in other words, provincial cities with many of the information resources of massive, melting-pot metropolises. If such places suffer from a "crisis in language," one way to fill the linguistic vacuum might be to use the noun *Albuquerque* as their metaphor. Albuquerque cities are those emerging cities of hybrid vigor that are reaching for a larger share of the migratory global economy, while struggling to preserve their local culture and sense of place.

In an Albuquerque city, using reputation and "image" as maps to true identity would be as misleading as using clothing to assess a person's character and moral fiber. The same is true, of course, for Albuquerque itself. To start making sense of Albuquerque as a unique locality, one needs to abandon

superficial appearances and experience some of the city's symbolic vantage points—Albuquerque at night from the air, the
view from the top of Nine Mile Hill, the zigzag neon of the
Beach Apartments, the messages of the old and new airports,
the home of architect Bart Prince, and the view of the city
from the perspective of the Rio Grande and its bosque.

Compared to its prewar small-town size and character,
Albuquerque has become a sprawling metroplex, a decen-
tralized urban field of daunting proportions. But even the
modern city's sprawling mass is lost in New Mexico's continental scale. Flying east into the Albuquerque Basin at night,
one can see firsthand what might be the city's most remarkable quality—that it stops. Albuquerque is still one of the
few major metropolitan areas that has a distinguishable edge.
As the plane approaches the city after crossing an ocean of
blackness, it is possible to see the first light, the actual place
where the blackness washes onto the first outcropping of elec-
tricity. If you're used to flying into Los Angeles, say, or any
big American city, spotting that first lonely light bulb can
have the effect of a revelation. It's immediately apparent that
Albuquerque is not merely a commercial oasis swallowed up
by a dead sea of neon suburbs. It is a discrete place, a human
enclave in the middle of a vast emptiness.

To drive home the reality of Albuquerque's presence in
New Mexico—containing, as it does, almost half the state's
population—one need only motor west at night on Interstate
40 to the top of Nine Mile Hill. There on the rim of the Albuquerque Basin, surrounded by the darkness of the desert, one
feels like an explorer who has come upon a lost city, a huge,
sparkling oasis of light. When I saw Albuquerque that way
for the first time, I experienced some of the startling awe that
Cortez must have felt when he looked down into the Valley of
Mexico and beheld the gleaming, whitewashed city of Teno-

chtitlan. Both first impressions share an intensity of surprise that's not to be forgotten.

Seeking sanctuary from the night, one can start to feel the tensions and incongruities of the Albuquerque oasis by driving east from Nine Mile Hill on West Central past the relics of Route 66's motel strip, with its Southwestern neon, cactus imagery, and Depression-era adobe kitsch. Down the hill, past the rural darkness of Atrisco and other venerable South Valley neighborhoods, one crosses the Rio Grande on a six-lane bridge that's in the same place where Spanish settlers forded the river in the sixteenth century. Bridge traffic at night in the 1990s is an assortment of old trucks and smart imports, RVs and U-Hauls, gray-primered Chevys ready for colors, souped-up low-riders with chrome-plated chain steering wheels and shiny engines, and the occasional patrol car cruising through the night like a trained shark sniffing for trouble.

After crossing the Central bridge, one is blasted by another kind of neon—a jazzy zigzagging of light, pulsing like charges of adrenalin across the Pueblo-modernist facade of the Beach Apartments. Designed by Albuquerque architect Antoine Predock, the Beach serves as a symbol of Albuquerque's puzzling identity. Predock describes it as "a big 74-unit low-rider, parked on the historic main street of our country, Highway 66." The site of the Beach "straddles a cultural fault line where the habitat of the West Central Cruiser meets the fairway of the white belts and white shoes of the Albuquerque Country Club." Predock considers the Beach "an abstraction of Highway 66 iconography" that deals with the "poetically loaded" context of the area. Combining allusions to the "poignant motels and cafés" of West Central with the "subdued quasi-Mediterranean averaging out" of the Country Club neighborhood's "stylistic drift" and a "Navajo blanket" graphic patterning on the building's facade, the Beach reflects Albuquerque's eclectic heritage.[15] And that makes the building both alluring and strangely alienating.

Its allure comes from its vitality. The Beach is complicated, risky, brimming with exuberance and sentiment. Its Taos Pueblo–like clustering of spaces, its neon razzmatazz, its hard-edge, trendy banding in pastel "Navajo" colors, make it a sort of George Gershwin building composed from the heart-felt themes of local culture. But the Beach's sophisticated imagery is alienating too, because, like Albuquerque, its reality needs to be explained to make much sense. The building, like the city, seems overloaded, its hybrid vigor almost too energetic. Its hard edges are unsettlingly opposed to the soft mysteries of the bosque and the river nearby. The Beach has a flatness and harshness about it that give it a feeling of being a back-lot set, as temporary as the logoed facades of swank shops in shopping malls. And yet its symbolic intentions, which embody a fusion of Albuquerque's idealized past with a utopian American future, give the building an ephemeral sort of substance too, a gestural identity that asserts its right to be.

Metaphoric buildings ancestral to the Beach still play an important part in Albuquerque's architectural present. And the city has at least one major public building constructed in the late 1980s that's loosely comparable to the Beach's postmodern gesture to Southwestern culture—the new Albuquerque Airport. Both the Beach and the new airport, as tropes of New Mexico's complexity, are linked directly to the sophisticated, Depression-era old Albuquerque Airport and its Spanish Pueblo Revival–style kin at the University of New Mexico and other places in town. Both buildings are also associated with the cartoonlike Pueblo motel and café architecture from the heyday of Route 66, when America's

"main street" went through the heart of the city and Albuquerque saw itself as a motorist's oasis. The city's business
community wanted travelers to remember Albuquerque. So
they took their lead from "high art" Southwestern style buildings at the train station, the old airport, and the university. As
with the Beach, merchants loaded their buildings with New
Mexican metaphors. To the vacationing motorist, the puebloesque exteriors of Route 66 motels must have seemed as exotic
and whimsically outlandish as the hat shape of Hollywood's
famous Brown Derby restaurant.

While the metaphors of the Beach allude to the history of
architecture in New Mexico, the old and new airports aren't
that much different in intention from the billboard architecture of New Mexican motels and cafés. Although the airports
are not designed to help sell a particular commercial product, the allusions they employ are meant to create a general
marketing image for Albuquerque. The old airport, though,
evokes a grander meaning—an emotional meaning—that the
new airport fails to achieve.

Completed in 1939, the old airport was designed by Er-
nest H. Blumenthal and funded by the WPA.[16] It is the only
WPA air terminal in the country built of steel and adobe in
the Pueblo Revival style.[17] For visitors to the outpost of New
Mexico, the old airport—with its adobe-colored cubic forms,
its carved vigas, flagstone floors, and giant fireplace—stood
as a monument to the foreignness of the state. And that's what
the designers of the new airport had hoped to achieve as well.
But when it comes to celebrating the underlying realities of
the Myth of New Mexico, the new airport stumbles.

The old airport, which still stands just west of the new
one, belongs to the genre of New Mexico architecture that
alludes directly to actual buildings and artifacts that form the
reality of New Mexican culture. The old airport not only

represents a serious regional style, it also serves an educational function. It helps maintain a knowledgable community enthusiasm for local culture. While the new airport has many practical virtues, it does not serve a similar function. It is not a symbolic gateway to the Land of Enchantment.

Designed by BPLW Architects and Engineers of Albuquerque, the $120 million new airport is owned and operated by the city of Albuquerque. It is an expansion and total remodeling of a 1965 version by William E. Burk, Jr., which incorporated much of the New Mexico feel of the 1939 WPA building. Dallas critic David Dillon wrote of Burk's design that it "makes one of America's great first impressions. . . . You know immediately that you're not in Dallas or Atlanta."[18] One might be able to say the same thing about the new airport, but not so much because it reflects New Mexico's mysterious character, but rather because it is merely different. As BPLW's lead designer, Ron Peters, was quoted as saying, "We want people to say: 'I've never been in an airport like this!' That's the city's main objective."[19]

The new airport makes numerous postmodern gestures to New Mexico regionalism. Its external shell is composed of a handsome massing of forms reminiscent of Pueblo buildings. But its spare use of Native American stepped-cloud motifs, its small divided windows, and its prefab stylized *latillas* (timber infill between beams), are references that are so minimized and arcane that only architectural scholars might enjoy them. The most obviously New Mexican parts of the new airport's interior are its permanent art exhibits and the carved and painted vigas in the Great Hall, which are left over from the 1965 building. Intelligently curated, the art collection is spread out through most of the airport and gives viewers a chance to sample the full range of the state's aesthetic culture—from Native American and Hispanic folk art to contemporary action painting. Overall, though, the new airport is an odd project of fashion. It has taken a pastel "Southwestern style" that was lifted from New Mexico and dolled up and popularized in department stores on the East and West coasts and brought it back to New Mexico, where it can't hope to compete with the real thing.[20]

Another of the city's symbolic vantage points is located in the heart of the university neighborhood. It's the eccentric home of the internationally respected Albuquerque architect Bart Prince. Prince's work belongs in the company of Barcelona architect Antonio Gaudi and Simon Rodilla, the genius of Watts Towers in Los Angeles. His buildings make no reference to New Mexico regionalism, yet they could be called indigenous. They reflect the technological and futuristic side of Albuquerque's Anglo-American culture. A native New Mexican, Bart Prince traces his aesthetic heritage through Frank Lloyd Wright and the renegade Oklahoma expressionist architect Bruce Goff. Whereas New Mexican regionalists use the forms and materials of Hispanic and Pueblo adobe structures, Prince's buildings combine organic shapes with space-age materials and machinery that one might find at the laser and nuclear weapons laboratories at Kirtland Air Force Base. Prince is an architect of ideas, a free thinker who, like Wright, sees no use in imitation. Just as regionalist architect John Gaw Meem synthesized the spirit of modernism with traditional Southwestern forms, so Bart Prince has synthesized the freedom, novelty, and individuality inherent in the frontier environment with the creative confidence of modernism and its liberating technology. Prince's own home seems like a living creature, a genetically engineered house that combines the luminosity of a Chinese lantern with the fantastic forms of a Jules Verne spaceship. It is both voluptuous and enigmatic, much like the modern city in which it exists.

V. B. Price

To round out the experience of Albuquerque's identity from a symbolic perspective, one should drive during the day north from Central Avenue on Coors Road west of the river, past the glitz of commercial strip developments, past the award-winning cluster of neo-adobe condominiums called La Luz, past the nuevo Burbank of Paradise Hills, down through the not-so-rural nonconformist haven of the village of Corrales, up onto Rio Rancho Road, down past the tract houses of the River's Edge development, and finally over open but platted range land to State Highway 44. A mile east from the intersection is the entrance to Coronado State Monument, which not only has a fine preconquest Pueblo ruin and a good museum, but also perhaps the most power-ful view to be had of both the Sandia Mountains and the Rio Grande. From a vantage point on the bluffs overlooking the river, one is confronted again with Albuquerque's essential nature. It is a city lost in a landscape, a full-fledged, main-stream American city, sprawling within a desert wilderness that's dominated by a chain of mountains and transformed into a fragrant and fertile Eden by the sixth greatest river in North America.

A short drive east on Highway 44 takes you to a bridge that spans the river and to the beginnings of the area's an-cient irrigation system, which runs for hundreds of miles, crisscrossing the North and South valleys. Walking on the ditches, one can directly experience the vitalizing influence of the river and the great trough, flood plain, and alluvium upon which Albuquerque sprawls. Until the mid 1980s, it didn't seem possible that Albuquerque could ever dominate its natural environment as other cities have come to do. But the possibility now can't be denied, though from the ditch banks it still seems unlikely. Looking east to the foothills of the Sandias over farmland with its patterns of trees, or over

the cottonwood bosque to the West Mesa sand hills and volcanoes, Albuquerque, once called "the blank wall capital of
the nation,"[21] seems almost invisible.

But such views are optical illusions, the soothing magic
of perspective. Albuquerque is not only its New Mexican
soul nor merely its hard and disagreeable exterior form. It
is everything it is. Architectural philosopher Robert Venturi
might say that Albuquerque's built environment is charged
with the "messy vitality" of the real as opposed to the "obvious unity" of the artificial.[22] Waspish design critic Peter Blake
might counter that Venturi's commitment to "existing conditions"[23] and popular culture, outlined in his famous book
Learning from Las Vegas, is a betrayal of civilized values that has
resulted in cities like Albuquerque, decked out in the cheap
finery and minimal expectations of "vulgarian chic."[24] While
Blake might cast Albuquerque as another modern American
urban excrescence, a junkyard city, seeing only the geode's
shell, Venturi might glorify the shell itself, convinced that the
geode's inner beauty was dependent upon its outward mess.

But Albuquerque is neither a junkyard nor a gambler's Val-
halla. It's not a failed mainstream clone, nor the All American dream town of TV commercials that promote its lawns
and hide its "mud huts" in pursuit of the El Dorado of economic development. It would be as inaccurate to say that
Albuquerque's identity is confined to its war-zone commercial strips as it would be to say that the military-industrial
complex, the city's largest employer, runs Albuquerque like a
company town. Nor, of course, is Albuquerque an idealized
Native American–Hispano metropolis, any more than it is a
Disneyized adobe tourist mecca like Santa Fe.

Albuquerque is in a depressing muddle. It has no sense
of purpose. No consensus on the future exists. The city is
addled by both its negative reputation and by the disorienting

miseries of rapid growth. Its national image as a provincial outback, a colonial territory, a place of no intrinsic value, a third-world city of cheap labor, low expectations, and mediocre clientele withers the city's self-confidence.

The more Albuquerque's collective spirit is seduced by its inaccurate reputations, the more it compromises its integrity as a New Mexican city. As Albuquerque seeks to identify itself with other mainstream cities and abandon self-reliance for the sake of understandable imitation, its shaping tensions and paradoxes are in danger of being replaced not by messy vitality, and not by vulgarian chic, but by a tragic and wasteful conformity that not only limits the city's economic potential but destroys its natural and historic environments.

3

Albuquerque and Santa Fe

F O R small and midsized cities in exotic localities that seek independence from the "progressive monoculture" of the twenty-first century,[1] the future holds two deeply troubling cultural and economic questions that must be answered. First, how can such cities grow and still maintain their identities as "authentic" places? And second, how can they preserve their authenticity—their sense of place—without trivializing it into a cultural commodity, transforming what ethnographic historian James Clifford calls "authentic human differences" into "collectible" art or folklore?[2] Coming to terms with these questions has much to do with the urban histories of modern Albuquerque and its cultural competitor, Santa Fe.

Both questions address a fundamental economic-development issue in the overurbanized and homogenizing planetary culture of the 1990s. To compete in an urban marketplace dominated by massive metroplexes, smaller exotic cities must maintain their quality of life to attract the new wealth that comes with business and residential immigrants from polluted and overcrowded urban centers. And quality of life, as a market niche, is determined to a large degree by aesthetic novelty, social calm, and a clean and healthy natural environment.

How to grow and develop without compromising or trivializing authenticity are problems that progressive leaders in Albuquerque and Santa Fe find painful and frustrating. Both cities have used historic preservation and enlightened, if inconsistent, land-use planning as bulwarks against homogenization and banality. Critics complain that Albuquerque hasn't done enough and that Santa Fe has gone too far. On the surface, both cities seem to have ruined themselves in the struggle to create a market niche. They have, nonetheless, made an effort. And the differences between them, and their approaches to growth and economic development, give useful clues for the creation of a general strategy for becoming competitive without being self-destructive.

Albuquerque and Santa Fe chose different futures for themselves and have had dramatically different circumstances to deal with since the coming of the railroad in 1880. They compete with each other for tourist dollars and cultural status. Residents of Santa Fe delight in bashing Albuquerque's working-class aura and industrial ambience. And Albuquerqueans happily admit to finding Santa Fe pretty, but unbearably chichi and small-town. Both cities have radically different self-images and polar-opposite national reputations. Albuquerque has always seen itself as a progressive city, while the nation has come to see it often as a squalid and backward place. And, indeed, Albuquerque is a full-fledged mid-sized major American city of over half a million inhabitants. Santa Fe still believes itself to be an art colony and cultural mecca that is incidentally a state capital of some sixty thousand people blessed with the best publicity in the last ten years of any small city in the country.

When it comes to the discrepancies between reputation and

identity, Santa Fe is as paradoxical as Albuquerque. While Santa Fe's positive reputation is not undeserved, it hides many deep social and cultural problems, much as Albuquerque's well-earned negative image masks the city's remarkable aesthetic and environmental assets. Santa Fe's modern reputation is that of a Southwestern version of Beverly Hills, the "in" city of the 1990s, a secret haven in which to hide far from the madding world—a sort of romantic, American cultural oasis complete with cowboys, Indians, señoritas, and a "style" all its own that clothiers, interior decorators, and perfume manufacturers can rely on to make them a fortune.

But Santa Fe has also been the object of harsh criticism in New Mexico. And much of it has to do with the trivialization of authentic culture and the gentrification that seems to have come with it. "We've painted our town brown, and moved our brown people out."[3] That's what city councilwoman and defeated mayoral candidate Debbie Jaramillo told the national press in 1989. She was referring to Santa Fe's Historic Styles zoning code which mandates adobe-style architecture for the city's historic core. Jaramillo, who championed a slow-growth policy, was defeated by progrowth Mayor Sam Pick. Jaramillo led a field of four slow-growth advocates whose combined votes would have beaten Pick. In a *USA Today* story, headlined "Santa Fe, a divided boom town," Jaramillo said she "thinks Santa Fe's selling itself as a 'trendy chic hot spot,' and selling out its residents in the process. 'We're just giving this town away.'"[4] Long-time Santa Fe author Richard Bradford commented that developers "say Santa Fe is enchanting. 'What they mean is they find it financially promising.'"[5] Roger Morris, a Santa Fe political writer and public television journalist, has observed, "You cannot long enjoy this place if social resentments and the bitterness of the community grow to such an extent that the charm and welcome that you first found as a visitor disappear after you build your million-dollar house."[6]

Gentrification in Santa Fe seems to have come hand in hand with the city's boom through the 1970s and 1980s, when the authenticity of its identity as a multicultural city also came into question. For me, the symbol of the displacement of working-class people in Santa Fe is a Hispanic woman I knew who could no longer afford to keep her family home in Santa Fe. In her late fifties, she moved to Albuquerque and commuted the 120-mile round trip to Santa Fe every day to her job as a chambermaid in one of the city's hotels. Working-class Hispanic residents are even under siege aesthetically. Brightly colored, eccentric vernacular houses built by their owners in the westside Guadalupe neighborhood are coming into conflict with Santa Fe's rigid zoning code. A thoroughly distinctive and evolving cultural landscape, the area has been invaded by the adobe coloration and multistory puebloesque buildings mandated under the Historic Styles ordinance. Architectural historian Beverley Spears has remarked that the

> underlying question behind these ordinance issues is whether the unique character of the westside neighborhood should be protected and encouraged, or the neighborhood should be either allowed to or forced to transform itself into the stereotypical Santa Fe look. . . .[7]

Such aesthetic issues come hand in hand with Santa Fe's "hot spot" reputation and the rapid turnover of real estate and the escalation of prices that has come with it.

In a copyrighted poll conducted by the *Albuquerque Journal* in early 1990, nearly 66 percent of Santa Fe's residents said the city was growing too fast, and that the attitude of local government toward developers was "too lenient." Some 53 percent felt that Santa Fe was becoming a "worse place to live," and only 23.8 percent thought it was getting better.[8] More telling, perhaps, is that in this celebrated city of three cultures, only slightly over half of those polled rated the "climate of racial and ethnic relations" excellent to good.[9]

Living in an architecturally beautiful city is apparently no longer good enough for most Santa Fe residents. The town's become just too big and just too rich, with housing costs at 38 percent above the national average. And even the reputation of its Spanish Pueblo–style buildings, which give the city its unique visual character and tourist appeal, has come under withering assault. No less a personage than the Dean of the School of Architecture and Planning at the University of New Mexico, George Anselevicius, has called the historic style "memory wall paper," complaining that it is "superficial and cosmetic."[10] That sentiment could surely be applied to the city as a whole if one knew of it only through its press clippings.

Santa Fe's national image as a celebrity oasis and exotic watering hole began to gather momentum in the early 1980s. In 1982 alone, articles appeared in *Rolling Stone*, *Time*, *Newsweek*, *Town and Country*, *National Geographic*, *Esquire*, and *Rocky Mountain Magazine*. And the language used to describe the city kept drifting into metaphors appropriate for fashion magazines. *Esquire*, for instance, described the City Different as being "a kiss promiscuous," though the hard-hitting *Rocky Mountain Magazine* "desanctified" Santa Fe, damning it for its "peon wages," "illusion of Nirvana," and "attitudes of many rich employers that seem to say 'Let 'em eat the mountains. . . . Let 'em eat the light.'"[11] Even the *National Geographic* succumbed to arch banalities, musing that "somewhere in the area, one knows, penitents are wounding themselves behind locked chapel doors. . . ."

Santa Fe has long been the butt of those who attack anything eccentric as being effete. But even in the 1960s it was relatively easy to defend Santa Fe as an authentic place, a city of oddballs perhaps, even a fantasyland, a Williamsburg of the Southwest, but not a public-relations sound stage in which props and facades are taken for reality. The late poet Winfield Townley Scott, a refugee from the East Coast who spent the last fourteen years of his life in Santa Fe, defended the city in a 1961 essay, writing that

> It is unavoidable that the significant attraction of Santa Fe brings in the escapee, the malcontent, the failure, the exhibitionist, the dubiously talented. Outsiders sometimes consider the place to be "full of frauds." It is not. There are many genuinely talented people who work steadily and quietly right along with the keepers of grocery stores and the ambitious young exploiters of uranium. Santa Fe is not an artist's colony; it is predominantly a workaday city with a full share of the kind of man Dorothy Parker once pined for—the kind "who solicits insurance."[12]

Cities, like people, are more than just their physical beings. They are subjective realities as well. They are, at once, what they think about themselves and what other people think about them. The Santa Fe of the 1960s was a city that many New Mexicans loved and loyally defended. Locals and transplants like Scott disliked negative comparisons between Santa Fe and Albuquerque that suggested the City Different was less than all things to all people. No one in the state really liked

it, though many agreed, when architectural critic Ian Nairn
wrote in his 1965 book *The American Landscape* that Albuquerque was "an honest whore" while Santa Fe was "a wife
who cheats."[13] But I've come to see those now-famous de-
scriptions as metaphors for the excesses that have under-
mined the physical identities of both cities. And some twenty
years later, they still hold true. A February 1990 editorial
in the *Albuquerque Tribune*, for instance, expanded the metaphors, alluding to the competition between the two, saying
that "Santa Fe is the Shangri-La of the Chic, the Capitol of
the Cultured, Recherché on the Rio Grande" while "Albuquerque, of course, is the Tsaritsyn of Tackiness, the Taj
Mahal of Truck Stops, the Lost City of the Low Brows."[14]

Albuquerque and Santa Fe are profoundly different kinds
of cities, and they are so, to a certain extent, by choice. Responding to changing circumstances at the turn of the century, both cities chose different futures, oblivious, of course,
to the unintended consequences their choices would eventually engender. Santa Fe chose to be a specialty city, a distinctly
New Mexican place, capitalizing on its exotic qualities and
committing itself to the economics of tourism. Albuquerque
chose to become the state's progressive city, an American
place, modern and up-to-date, committing itself to an eclectic economy, keeping its options open for any kind of growth
that came along. Santa Fe chose directions that guaranteed
it would remain a small city. Albuquerque saw in its future
the possibility of becoming a major metropolis in the West.
By choosing to emphasize its New Mexican assets, Santa
Fe made a decision to direct its growth. Although it can't
be said that Albuquerque chose to grow without a plan, its
growth strategies never had Santa Fe's sharp focus. Albuquerque grew in response to market forces, with a minimum
of planning until after World War II. Albuquerque didn't so

much choose against its New Mexican character as it allowed
development to overwhelm it. Santa Fe didn't choose to become overgentrified and too pricey for many of its long-time
residents. Santa Fe became the victim of its popularity, of its
own extraordinarily successful image-making efforts.

When it comes to preserving quality of life and sense of
place through the 1990s, both Albuquerque and Santa Fe are
in danger of losing their great promise. They have both fallen
prey to an excess of their virtues. Not wanting to impede
the march of progress, Albuquerque didn't exercise enough
control over its growth. It could not restrain itself from welcoming any and all development that came its way. Santa Fe,
on the other hand, chose to fine-tune its public policies so
exactly that they haven't left room for the ethnic and socioeconomic diversity that the city's reputation is based on.

In 1912, Santa Fe's leaders looked to a combination of architectural regionalism and historic preservation as their major
economic-development strategy. Later, the city adopted strict
design and land-use codes to protect Santa Fe's romantic
image. It wasn't until the early 1970s that Albuquerque turned
to historic preservation and open-space planning as a way of
shoring up its quality of life and attracting its share of up-
wardly mobile young Sunbelt immigrants.

The railroad's presence in the 1880s caused both Albuquerque's early booming growth and Santa Fe's decline as a
major commercial center. While the railroad tracks ran only
a mile east of Old Town in Albuquerque, Santa Fe was by-
passed and connected to the mainline by an eighteen-mile-
long spur. This put the city at such a disadvantage that it
lost more than 10 percent of its population before statehood
in 1912.[15] That year, city officials made a conscious decision
for Santa Fe to become a tourist destination. "To accomplish
this," writes architectural historian Chris Wilson, "they pro-

posed the preservation of what remained of the historic town and the use of the Santa Fe style for all new construction." [16] Civic leaders were also concerned with preserving the city's winding old streets and developing an overall urban plan. But it was left to archaeologists and historians at the Museum of New Mexico to define the qualities of the Santa Fe style. One of the leaders, the distinguished Mayanist Sylvanus G. Morley, proposed a planning ordinance that would turn Santa Fe into a "Glorified Adobe City" and "the tourist center of the Southwest." [17] It's a telling point that while Santa Fe was in the throes of starting up what Chris Wilson calls "the business of cultural image making" [18] through design and preservation, the University of New Mexico in Albuquerque in 1909 fired its innovative president, William George Tight, in part for filling the campus with Spanish Pueblo-style buildings. "The excuse was that he had fired two faculty members without consulting the Board [of Regents], but the real cause was his architectural indiscretion." [19]

New Mexico seems at times to be obsessed with architecture. The decisions of 1912 in Santa Fe have fueled an ongoing debate about architectural style that troubles the city to this day. To its detractors, Santa Fe's uniform design code of 1957 has turned it into an Adobeland of fake Pueblo architecture and mock culture. And Albuquerque's firing of President Tight signaled the beginning of a century-long struggle to find and preserve a niche for itself in the architectural history of the state.

The battle over architecture in both cities pits progressives and modernists against cultural conservatives and romantics. Romanticism has won in Santa Fe just as progressivism has won in Albuquerque. And both victors have gone too far in consolidating their power. A glimpse of the architecture war at its highest levels was given to the readers of *New Mexico*

Architecture magazine in 1962 when it ran a conversation with Lewis Mumford, America's greatest urban thinker, and John Gaw Meem, New Mexico's greatest exponent and defender of romantic architecture.

Mumford took exception to Santa Fe's rigid design codes, saying he saw no reason "why there shouldn't be considerable latitude in the development of regional architecture" in the city. He added that it was "very dangerous to lay down by ordinance a fixed style. That's the way to kill the development of architecture." Referring to Santa Fe's tendency to cover over its stock of nineteenth-century Italianate and neo-classical office buildings with adobe brown stucco and puebloesque facades, Mumford said pointedly that he "would certainly have preserved . . . in Santa Fe some of the buildings of the middle nineteenth century that have been destroyed. . . . You destroy the memory of the past if you ruthlessly wipe out all buildings of an earlier period in order to make the city look more uniform than any really living community should look." Mumford felt strongly that architects who "design flagrantly non-regional buildings" that ignore the climate and "various other aspects of the scene, shouldn't be encouraged. But neither should people be commanded by law to produce fakes—mere superficial imitations of what was done honestly in the past."[20]

John Gaw Meem, the master architect of UNM's Spanish Pueblo style in its heyday from the 1930s to the late 1950s, and for years the arbiter of architectural taste in Santa Fe, took profound exception to Mumford's comments, especially his use of the word *fake*. Meem thought it was all a "misconception." "You can call it fake to make these buildings look like adobe if you want to, but there are certain elemental forms connected with them that to me seem to tie the buildings into a tradition. One uses these forms symbolically, so to speak." Santa Fe had a "problem with conservation," Meem maintained. "I therefore think that it is absolutely legitimate for Santa Fe to have an Historical Zone in the center of the city where the majority of the older buildings are." Meem was both subtle and passionate about his opposition to rigid ideological modernism.

> I regret having it called "fake" architecture, because architecture should be very flexible. And for the sake of joy, of recollection, of familiarity, I think the architecture should be free to—shall we say—to violate certain material functional requirements. There are many great periods in architecture where certain functional requirements have been violated for the sake of the spirit. . . . I don't feel that we are doing something that is wrong, something that is reprehensible. . . . It is possible to produce delightful, comfortable buildings inside this general pattern.[21]

Mumford countered with a final objection to making modern buildings, with modern functions—such as gas stations and department stores—conform to a historic pattern. "But I do not see any way, without actually caricaturing the very thing we wish to preserve, of making new buildings conform to an obsolete pattern."[22]

It is the dual charge of caricaturing tradition and failing to create "a really living community" that has undercut the effectiveness of Santa Fe's cultural image making during the boom years of the 1980s. Meem's argument, on the other hand, foreshadowed the postmodern revolt against dictatorial modernism. Meem held, and rightly in my view, that architecture can and should have cultural meaning over and above its functional utility. And while Meem's buildings themselves were never caricatures, the Spanish Pueblo Revival style itself is vulnerable to the same charge of being cosmetic and trivial as that leveled at historically ornamented postmodern buildings in the 1980s. Still, until recently, I have always found the core of Santa Fe to be a beautiful and comforting urban space. Its evocations of New Mexican culture used to make romantics like myself feel warmly at home. And even now, despite the alienating rise of commercialism and the city's status as a haven for the rich and famous, Santa Fe represents an ultimate achievement of what contemporary German architect Wilhelm Kücker calls architecture as the "art of staging."[23] Santa Fe has always seemed to me like a stage set, or, more appropriate to its founding fathers at the Museum of New Mexico, an architectural diorama. At a design conference in Bonn in 1988, Kücker opened his speech on "Architecture as Back Drop" by asking, "Has city architecture ever been anything but the art of stage setting, of presentation of whatever the contemporary idea of urbanity happened to be?"[24] But Kücker attacks the notion of architecture as merely facade, background, theater, and "entertainment." Like much criticism directed at Santa Fe, his view of the postmodern discovery of the "entertainment value of architecture" is witheringly harsh. "Authenticity is not in demand where the emphasis is merely on the production of images which are however supposed to simulate yesterday's authenticity." Such "cultivation of the urban image," he maintains, "has little to do with the discovery of historical identity. It mainly serves commerce," tarting up buildings in "shameless competition for vanishing purchasing power. . . ."[25] Meem, of course, would have taken strong exception to such criticism.

Cities cannot help being settings. As contexts in which urban life takes place, they can be objects of architectural high fashion or of strict utility, or the byproducts of organizational anarchy. But they are always settings. Santa Fe chose to design itself, to accentuate its vision of cultural pluralism in New Mexico. "Fake" or not, the originality of its architectural illusions and the uniqueness of its romantic spirit satisfy the imagination like few urban environments in North America. Santa Fe is a real place. It chose a cultural image as its reality. That image was not only an ingenious marketing tool; it used to be an object of pride for the city's residents. In the 1980s, however, the city's character changed. The motives of pride and identity were submerged in the hugely successful commercial exploitation of the city's romantic imagery. The historic core of the city increasingly became not a stage setting for urban life, but an elaborate storefront for high-priced tourist goods. When the downtown core losts its department store, its drug store, and other "real-life" retailers, it also lost its real-life urban clientele. It became more, indeed, like a Pueblo Disneyland than a "really living," romantic New Mexican city.

While Santa Fe has been concerned mostly with the art of staging, Albuquerque never paid enough attention to the feelings evoked by its physical image. Although Albuquerque's well-to-do have long delighted in importing the latest architectural fashions, and could even be said to take a collector's interest in architecture as an art form, the city's leadership was never interested in creating a unified urban image to rival Santa Fe's. In fact, for a city with such an interest in building and design, Albuquerque has had a perverse zest for demolition. Santa Fe destroyed many of its historic buildings by covering them up; Albuquerque just tore them down. As a result, Albuquerque is a city with amnesia, a place with a fascinating past and almost no collective memory. It committed a cultural lobotomy on itself from the mid 1950s to the early

1970s when it permitted the destruction of hundreds of its historic properties. In the mid 1950s, the downtown core was a tiny architectural museum, packed with a small but select number of wonderful buildings. At the west end of Central Avenue, for instance, was a Masonic Temple based on the Parthenon which sat side by side with what some European critics considered to be one of the more famous buildings in America—a multistory Pueblo Revival–style hotel, built on the model of Taos Pueblo, called the Franciscan. Today, the site of those buildings is still occupied by a block-long parking lot.

Unlike Santa Fe's, Albuquerque's leadership could not agree on a single economic-development strategy. While buildings downtown were being demolished to make room for urban renewal, a preservation lobby was urging the creation of a historic district in Old Town, which the city mandated in 1957. But preservationists didn't become a powerful force until 1971, after downtown's two world-class historic hotels—the Pueblo Franciscan and the California Mission–style Alvarado, a city landmark since 1902—had been leveled. In the space of less than two years, downtown Albuquerque had lost its best chance to become a major attraction for travelers and conventioneers. If Albuquerque's fragmented leadership could have formed a consensus at the end of World War II to accommodate growth while preserving the downtown's unique identity, New Mexico would have two major "historic cities," one a diorama of Southwestern imagery and cultural mythology, the other a Western American downtown complete with adobe hotels, 1920s neo-classical style banks, and a 1950s curtain wall skyscraper. Albuquerque's expanded Convention Center and new Hyatt Hotel would have had three luxury Southwestern hotels surrounding them—the Territorial-Style old Hilton, now renamed La Posada, the Alvarado, and the Franciscan—all of them powerful draws for visitors, one-of-a-kind places you remember and write home about. And the remaining significant historic properties downtown—the Pueblo Deco Kimo Theatre, the white tile replica of the Doge's Palace in Venice, the Italianate Sunshine office building, to name a few—would have been surrounded by a vibrant urban context. They would be important parts of Albuquerque's image and identity rather than beautiful but isolated oddities that one must make a special effort to find.

Albuquerque is no longer the architectural museum it once was. But, ironically, even with urban renewal, it still has more intact examples of America's frontier architectural past than Santa Fe. The city's 1978 historic-preservation ordinance protected most of Albuquerque's remaining stock of historic buildings, all of which are concentrated in the Old Town/Downtown urban core and its surrounding North and South Valley neighborhoods. A 1987 draft of a Comprehensive Historic Preservation Plan lists more than 200 buildings and districts that are either on the State Register of Cultural Properties, on the National Register of Historic Places, or are designated as City Landmarks. The list of historic buildings includes such diverse structures as a venerable one-story adobe hacienda from the prerailroad era known as the Barela de Bledsoe House, the Mayan-detailed Springer Office Building near downtown, the Academic Gothic brick compound of the old Albuquerque High School and the International Style Lembke House with its rounded forms and glass brick windows.

If Albuquerque's historic properties were not dispersed and hidden among the architectural byproducts of more than a hundred years of steady and sometimes booming growth, the city's approach to preservation would seem enlightened com-

pared to Santa Fe's. When Albuquerque first decided in 1957
to make Old Town into a historic zone, it did so partially in
response to Santa Fe–like attempts to "puebloize" a number
of Victorian buildings around the plaza. While Old Town is
largely a tourist attraction, playing a minimal role in Albuquerque's image of itself and unvisited by most residents, it
has retained much of the eclecticism that distinguishes Albuquerque from Santa Fe. And it contains the oldest major
landmark still standing in the city—San Felipe de Neri—
which is, itself, a varitable icon of eclecticism. Built on the
north side of the plaza in 1793, the church has served its
parish for nearly 200 years. Made of terrones—rectangu-
lar, sun-dried bricks cut from sod that make extra-thick,
strong walls—the church has undergone a steady metamorphosis, reflecting the changing tastes of its parishioners and
priests. Few objects in New Mexico are as ethereal and imposing as San Felipe's twin wooden "folk gothic" bell towers,
added in the 1850s. They rise above Old Town as signals to
the observant that there's something more to Albuquerque
than its dominating concrete, fast-food, car-culture image.
One can see the wooden spires from just about anywhere
in the Old Town vacinity. They look almost exactly as they
do in a photograph of the church taken in the 1870s. The
towers, along with the front of the church are the result of
a nineteenth-century Europeanization of the original structure.[26] Even today, with cast concrete rock exterior wainscot
around the front door of the building, which came in conflict
with the Old Town Historic Zone design requirements in the
1970s, San Felipe is a revealing clue to Albuquerque's eccentricity. The fake stone, pleasing to parishioners, signifies that
San Felipe is a working parish and not a museum for tourists.

The preservation of Old Town has not resulted in gentrification of surrounding neighborhoods. The Old Town His-

toric Zone ordinance is not, like Santa Fe's, a rigid design
code that stipulates exactly how buildings must look, right
down to the window sizes. The Old Town code is based
loosely on historic styles that existed in the city before 1900.
It requires new buildings in the district to conform to general
patterns rather than reproduce precise detailing. Old Town is
a historic enclave in the middle of a modern city that it has no
hope or intention of influencing. Santa Fe's historic core has
shaped and influenced the form of the entire city since 1912.

There is much to learn from both cities when it comes
to managing change. As an economic-development strategy,
Santa Fe chose to resist physical change, freezing its urban
form and architectural image to attract tourists and an affluent
real estate clientele. This has proven to be a most successful
approach. But business and government leaders in Santa Fe—
who were mostly Anglo-American—also created a city that
they themselves enjoyed living in, a city whose outward form
corresponded to their own romantic mythology of the Southwest. The gentrification of Santa Fe seems not to have been
a conscious part of the economic-development plan. It oc-
curred when Santa Fe's image as a remote and beautifully
exotic city appealed to larger numbers of wealthy Americans
who could afford to leave the cultural anonymity of big-city
suburban life and find refuge in New Mexico.

Albuquerque grew and developed under totally different
circumstances. Unlike Santa Fe, it did not have to compensate
for a loss of business when the railroad came. It embraced its
good fortune and grew as quickly and profitably as it could.
It did little or nothing to control its growth until the 1950s.
And in the forty-five years since the end of World War II, it
has, despite strong efforts from urban activists and planners,
radically detached itself from the romantic image of New
Mexico, once the bread and butter of most cities in the state.

Santa Fe's persistent continuity with the myth of New Mexico was a business decision. It has given Santa Fe a distinctive market niche in the competitive atmosphere of mobile urban America. Albuquerque's leadership came to agree that the town could achieve economic success by competing as a mainstream, modern American city. Although part of its leadership clung to the area's New Mexican roots—through historic preservation, arts activism, museum construction, and open-space creation—Albuquerque's business community generally believed that it could overcome New Mexico's remoteness and culturally benighted image and do successful combat with Denver, Phoenix, and other rising Sunbelt powerhouses.

Albuquerque's economic-development strategies have not been as realistic, or as successful, as Santa Fe's because New Mexico's foreignness and eccentricity cannot be overcome. Trying to take New Mexico out of Albuquerque is as futile as trying to take Japan out of Tokyo. Albuquerque is not in the blighted mainstream of urban America. And that's among its greatest assets in competing for new light industry and corporate headquarters. To boost its chances for more and better jobs, Albuquerque must, I think, embrace its New Mexican identity and look for new residents and businesses that want to locate in a city with a distinct and self-respecting sense of place, a city that prides itself upon its cultural and ecological integrity without being small-minded and reluctant to mature.

Modernism and Regionalism

I F Albuquerque has an indigenous skyline, it exists in perception from a shaded vantage point on Yale Boulevard on the University of New Mexico campus. Looking northeast from beneath the trees around the old Biology Building, one can see a great cluster, almost a mountain, of New Mexican buildings. Most are modernist buildings, unornamented, but colored "earth tone" brown. And crowning the architectural mountain is the famous form of Zimmerman Library, arguably the grandest expression of Spanish Pueblo Revival–style architecture in the state. These buildings all belong together. They represent stylistic opposites, even antagonists, that have been reconciled into a potent synthesis, a symbol of what architectural historian Edna Heatherington has called Albuquerque's singular urban condition—that of being at the crossroads of the ancient and the up-to-date. Although regionalism is Albuquerque's significant contribution to world architecture, as Heatherington says,[1] Albuquerque has never unanimously approved it. But the UNM campus cancels confrontation. It is at once a modernist and regionalist enclave, a place in which the imaginative sterility of pure function has been given new life by an infusing of symbolic content.

59

A work of architecture is more than merely the form of its functions. What is often dismissed as style and ornamental forms in buildings—domes and arches in modern Egypt, for instance, or the circular kivas and D-shaped city-houses of the Anasazi—have become, over time, symbols of cultural identity. Architecture can not only embody the spirit of an age, it can stand for the spirit of a particular place and people.

In Albuquerque, and New Mexico, the long history of architectural wrangling over matters of style, aesthetic ideology, and "taste" masks deeper concerns about the preservation of local culture. Architecture practiced by architects and architecture practiced by "the people," building in vernacular styles, have different relationships to symbolic function. In New Mexico, the tenacious roots of vernacular preference have prevailed to create a symbolic sense of place that mirrors the cultural identity maintained in Pueblo and Hispanic village life.

Almost separately, however, formal architecture—architecture by artist-professionals—has been the battleground in New Mexico for a studied, and some would say artificial, confrontation between modern internationalists, those concerned with universal function, and modern regionalists and revival-style architects, those forerunners of postmodernism who were concerned with integrating a vernacular sense of place into a modern urban environment. Much revival-style architecture in New Mexico was done to create a tourist-consumer environment. But its best work was carried out by Anglo-American and other romantics who wanted to honor and identify with the cultural mysteries of New Mexico.[2] At the University of New Mexico, architect John Gaw Meem made vernacular-style buildings that anyone could use, giving students and faculty the chance to inhabit and be influenced by forms that still embodied Pueblo and Hispanic cultures

flourishing in surrounding villages. The New Mexican sense
of place is so powerful that when regionalism came into conflict with modernism in the 1950s, the elegant simplicities of
regionalism, particularly on the campus at the University of
New Mexico, forced modernism to adapt itself to the local
sense of place and create a useful synthesis, a regional modernism, if you will.

This synthesis makes perfect sense. The New Mexican vernacular, its revivalist translations, and modernism are all expressions of practicality and honest function. While modernists, however, chose to deny the existence of style in their
work, revivalists realized that vernacular style took nothing
away from the dicta of function, but instead reinforced the
symbolic, emotional function of architecture in preserving
a cultural sense of place. Eventually, at UNM in particular,
functionally neutral modernist forms were used for the same
cultural purpose only in a stylistically more abstract way. The
creation of this synthesis has important implications.

The human world of the twenty-first century seems caught
between two dominant and conflicting forces: first, the desperate need to minimize human conflict by using modern
technology to help establish a worldwide community of em-
pathy and cooperation; and second, the urgent struggle on
the part of minority cultures and fragile ethnic environments
to protect themselves from the homogenizing influence of
power struggles between world states and great religions.
As a frontier contact zone since the sixteenth century, Albuquerque and New Mexico have had long and intimate experience with local cultures battling against world powers to
preserve their ethnic and political identities. From the Spanish conquest to the coming of the railroad, from the creation
of a regional architecture to the invasion of modernism, the
history of Albuquerque can be looked upon as a particularly

useful mirror of the future. For the better part of this century, internationalism and regionalism, modern technologies and specific cultural forms, the vernacular and the modern, have produced a stylistic, and necessarily symbolic, architectural hybrid vigor unique in the United States. In the harmony between modernism and the Spanish Pueblo Revival style, there is an important lesson for the future world's effort to make use of modern functions and contemporary know-how to reinforce and perhaps help develop a heterogeneous, eclectic world society. It is in this context of symbolic material culture that architecture in Albuquerque has been in the invisible avant-garde for more than eighty years, so far ahead of its time that it has seemed to various European and American sophisticates to be hopelessly backward and retarded. During the city's incessant growth from 1880 to the present, architecture has been the safe arena in which the battle between the "progressive" and the "provincial," the "first" and "third" worlds could take place.

But there's an odd twist to all this learning, too. While both regionalists and modernists profited from the vernacular preference for a sense of place, filling exclusive parts of Albuquerque, and virtually all of Santa Fe, with domestic imitations of rural utopia, "first-world" government housing on most Indian reservations in New Mexico makes no reference to either Pueblo architecture or revivalist evocations. Not only are there no symbolic gestures in government housing, there is no acknowledgment of the crucial role architecture and urban planning play in maintaining social solidarity. Most government housing has suburbanized Pueblo cities with single-family dwellings that have no room for traditional extended families and that are scattered around the periphery of urban cores, siphoning people and community focus away from the social unity of Pueblo life.[3] Moreover, the BIA houses I'm familiar with are a cross between California Ranch style and Boarding School Bungalow. What's worse is that they are made from "first-world" materials that take money rather than labor, traditional materials, and know-how to repair. Albuquerque and New Mexico's unique architectural history may offer important lessons for the future of a vigorous and heterogeneous world society, but, sadly, third-world Indian New Mexico itself, which is economically and bureaucratically oppressed, will probably never be a beneficiary.

If there's a perversity to the situation in New Mexico it's compounded by the social idealism of the modernist movement. This is not to say that government housing in Pueblos is the fault of modernism. But American bureaucratic culture, based on the principles of equity and reasonableness dear to the modern spirit, could not respond with modernist flexibility in its own outback. The formal lessons learned from the Hispanic and Indian vernacular that were translated by revivalist architects and then adapted by modernist architects concerned with contextual sensitivity were never picked up by the rationalist, engineering mentality of government agencies. So, style, symbol, and function in contemporary New Mexican architectural culture are all trapped in a socioeconomic dead-end. The social idealism of the modernist movement—to improve the world through design—is as much a creature of fashion, status, and monied isolation as the "ornamented" and "decorative" facades of the Santa Fe style. Neither revivalism nor modernism in New Mexico— both practiced with philosophical zeal—has been of much cultural use to the vernacular founders of the state's architectural heritage. Though it must also be said that architects of both persuasions have for years played an indispensable role in preserving architectural landmarks in Hispanic and Pueblo villages. So, while locked up in the economics of architecture, the lessons of hybrid vigor remain for those with the wit to put them to use.

The present governmental indifference to the success of regional design by both modernists and revivalists in New Mexico is consistent with the forces of "normalcy" and Americanization that have battled with the vernacular since New Mexico became a U.S. territory in 1846. Fashionable architecture, be it Queen Anne residences or Miesian skyscrapers, has held a fascination for all who have seen themselves as somehow stranded in the New Mexican outback. Stylish buildings and stylish clothing both give one the feeling of being liberated from the deprivations of the provinces. But there were romantics, too, who liked backward, mudhutted New Mexico more than the trendy, European-looking culture of the rest of the nation. And two such men—architect Edward B. Cristy and UNM president William George Tight—set the foundation for what would come to be the indigenous New Mexican skyline of UNM's central campus in the 1980s. Both men traditionally have been given credit for originating the Pueblo Revival style in New Mexico, though similar work had been carried out earlier and on a smaller scale in California and Arizona.

Tight and Cristy were men of great vision. At the turn of the century, they set in motion an architectural tradition that would result in what must be considered among the nation's great college campuses. UNM could be nowhere else but in New Mexico. Its strength, its intimacy, its individuality are all derived from the New Mexican land and the history of its people. No other campus in the country is so deeply rooted in its region's pre-Columbian and postconquest history. While other university villages around the nation looked to classical, Gothic, and Mediterranean architectural models, UNM, be-

fore 1910, was already coming to be a "pueblo on the mesa."
In 1927, the Spanish Pueblo Revival style was mandated by
the university's regents as the official style of the campus.
And by 1961, when modernist buildings first appeared on
campus, the regional style was so dominant that functionalist
architects adapted their designs to its essential forms.

The struggles between progressives and regionalists, between those who wanted to bring New Mexico up to snuff
and those who thought the place was a utopia as it was, have
made the UNM campus an object of controversy for most
of this century. In the 1950s, Frank Lloyd Wright, then in
his late eighties and dean of American architecture, went so
far as to call the campus "unfortunate" and "base." [4] And one
wag, after the turn of the century, wrote to the local papers
saying it made about as much sense as "clothing professors
and students in Indian shawls and breech cloths." [5]

What had folks alternately upset and sentimental is tied up
in terms that are confusing to almost everyone. UNM revival-
style architecture can be broken down into two major groups:
Pueblo Revival, sometimes known as Modified Pueblo, and
Spanish Pueblo Revival, both of which are a fusion between
Pueblo forms and those of Spanish mission churches. Modernist buildings on campus might be called "nuevo UNM,"
connoting a synthesis between revival styles and the sup-
posedly styleless functionalist aesthetic. In Santa Fe, revivalism is generally known as the Santa Fe style which incorpo-
rates elements of the Spanish Pueblo style and the Territorial
style, a basically adobe form often with brick coping and
Greek Revival detail. In Santa Fe today, buildings that have
the faintest whiff of nuevo UNM about them, such as the
mid-1980s adobe bunker of the First Interstate Bank building
at Lincoln and Marcy, are savagely attacked by revival-style
purists and others who know *schlock arkitektur* when they see it.

While the notion of designing buildings based on Pueblo forms had intrigued some romantics as early as 1887 (it was foreshadowed in an exhibition entitled "Cliff Dwellers" at the 1893 World's Columbian Exposition in Chicago and used at the famous Fred Harvey Hopi House at the Grand Canyon in 1904), it is unclear if either architect Cristy or President Tight were influenced by these earlier developments.[6] Tight came to New Mexico in 1901. A year later, the Fred Harvey Company built the California Mission–style Alvarado Hotel. Revivalism was in the air. Tight commissioned Cristy to visit Pueblo sites, including Hopi, Zuni, and Acoma. Cristy also examined plans of Anasazi ruins recorded by archaeologist J. Walter Fewkes. From 1905 to 1909, the two men—as architect and inspired client—collaborated to produce the first major institutional Pueblo Revival–style buildings. It was a daring break with prevailing tastes and trends in Albuquerque, which were dominated by various Victorian, eclectic, Romanesque, and beaux-arts styles. Cristy and Tight worked with both Pueblo and Spanish forms, creating a central heating plant, men's and women's dormitories, and a kivalike building for a fraternity (which can still be seen on University Boulevard near Grand). They also remodeled, or puebloized—as some people call it, "earlied up"—the largest building on campus, a Romanesque brick structure that would be called Hodgin Hall. The building—which serves as both a regional monument and as a butt of modernist criticism for being "dishonest" and cosmetic—is today one of the university's most honored historic buildings. Tight and Cristy's work was both so notorious and so successful that by 1907 a magazine writer had already labeled UNM a "Pueblo University."[7] Needless to say, such an environment was unique in North America.

Spanish Pueblo Revival–style buildings at UNM—based in large measure on developments in Santa Fe—appeared fully developed during the Depression when John Gaw Meem became the school's principal architect. Using Hispanic forms and Pueblo massing, popularized in Santa Fe's Fine Arts Building and Saint Francis Auditorium nearly two decades before, Meem produced masterworks with funds from the Works Progress Administration. In 1934 the administration building, now called Scholes Hall, was built; then the old Student Union Building, now the core of the anthropology complex, was completed in 1936; Zimmerman Library was finished a year later. By the time Bandelier Hall went up in 1941, Meem's influence was indelibly fixed on the campus. Meem served as UNM's only architect for twenty-five years. More than forty buildings bear his touch, including Mesa Vista Hall, Hokona Hall, and the old Johnson Gym.

The Spanish Pueblo Revival style was largely catalyzed by three building projects in Santa Fe: the 1909 restoration of the single-story, portaled Palace of the Governors; the mission church forms of Isaac Hamilton Rapp's 1916 Fine Arts Museum; and the stacked, modular Pueblo-like forms of the 1917 Santa Fe School for the Deaf. Both the Fine Arts Museum and Meem's major buildings at UNM were inspired by the mission church at Acoma. Meem, himself, had been instrumental in the restoration of the Acoma church and its twin towers in 1924 and 1925.[8]

While the Spanish Pueblo style in Santa Fe, including Meem's addition to the La Fonda Hotel in 1929, seems romanticized and rustic, coated with bumpy stucco and every kind of Hispanic and Pueblo design motif, Meem's work at UNM has a simpler, cleaner quality. In Zimmerman Library and Scholes Hall, Meem employed romantic detail, but in a mannered way, and refined the massive wall shapes of the churches into more abstract and geometric forms. Meem wrote that though his handling of the revival style was a "conscious recollection of the past," he never intended it to be "crystallized into an archaeological style."⁹

Meem retired in 1958. Five years later, Van Dorn Hooker, who had worked in Meem's office, became the official university architect at UNM. That same year, the first structure to break with revival-style tradition at UNM—the Education Complex by the Albuquerque functionalist office of Flatow, Moore, Bryan, and Fairburn—was completed. As President Tight had been attacked for borrowing from the past, the Education Complex was attacked for not borrowing enough. But even the Flatow firm, which took an engineering approach to design, adapted itself to the regional tone of the campus, by incorporating, among other elements, cast concrete Corbels, open court yards, and a kiva-shaped auditorium. The Education Complex came at the beginning of a twenty-five-year-long building program, which saw a remarkable and positive integration between regional styles and modernist principles. Under the direction of Van Dorn Hooker, modernist architects filled the campus with respectful but contemporary buildings, refining over the years an interdisciplinary genre which could be called either a regional or a contextual modernism. But it was Meem, the modern architect with regional sensibilities, who paved the way.

Meem was "much less concerned with invention and self-expression . . . than with the elaboration and perfection of existing traditions," wrote architect George Pearl in a lecture given in honor of Meem after his death in 1983. "His buildings were contextual for more than a generation before architectural critics began to write about context as a primary and most humane source of architectural character and form," Pearl wrote.¹⁰ By refusing to make the Spanish Pueblo Revival style an "archaeological" building type,

Meem led the way for it to become a medium of integration between the functionalist spirit of the modern age and the traditional and symbolic forms of vernacular architecture. To my thinking, that was Meem's most important contribution to world architecture. He demonstrated, as he said, that "old forms" could be used "for new buildings," that the cultural reinforcement and psychological assurance of architectural symbols need not be abandoned for efficiency and egalitarian ideals. Meem's regional buildings—the forerunners of contextual modernism and the best aspects of postmodernism—are in spirit more universal than the functional, styleless, unornamented, "work anywhere" machines of the International School. Meem's buildings clearly show that the virtue of functionalist architecture is not its fashionable emptiness, its monumental reductionist aesthetic, but rather its imageless flexibility, its very blankness, which permits it to be adapted, in varying degrees of intensity and content, to serve not only utilitarian needs but also the symbolic needs of local cultures around the world.

In a seminal article entitled "Old Forms for New Buildings," that appeared in the November 1934 issue of *American Architect and Architecture*, Meem linked Eliel Saarinen's view of modern architecture as expressing the cultural composite of "the fundamental form of time" with our era's "devotion of the ideal of scientific truth." He wrote:

> I like to think that the reason a good modern building is so logical, so clean and so honest is because it could not be otherwise in view of the high standards of uncompromising truth which science has set for itself—standards which constitute one of the great spiritual concepts of our day.[11]

He then forged a link between the honest function of vernacular architecture in the Pueblo/Hispanic Southwest and
the "fundamental form" of the modern age. "Some old forms
are so honest, so completely logical and native to the environment that one finds—to one's delight and surprise—that
modern problems can be solved, and are best solved by use
of forms based on tradition." He continued by saying that the

> value of this use may be questioned by some; but to me
> it seems to add a richness and actually to enhance a series
> of values. In a world tending more and more toward
> inevitable standardization—welcomed from the practi-
> cal point of view, but spiritually repugnant to us—it is
> truly refreshing to feel that in our contemporary archi-
> tectural movement [there] is still an opportunity for the
> expression of ancient values.

Meem summed up his view with a thoughtful question and
an emphatic answer.

> Is the effort of local architects to perpetuate ancient tra-
> ditional forms associated with their own region a sound
> one? The answer is, emphatically, yes! Particularly in
> the Southwest, architects who use old forms need do
> no violence to the ideals of contemporary architectural
> thought. On the contrary, the fundamental form of the
> time can best be expressed in a language native to the
> region.

Then he proclaimed what might well serve as the motto for
contextual modernism in the twenty-first century: "These
ancient shapes are modern! Evolved honestly within the limi-

tations of available materials, they are equally as well adapted to the new materials of our own day . . . ."

In the 1950s, when modernist architecture gained ascendancy in Albuquerque, Meem's work became controversial. UNM was seen as the last bastion of regionalism, and regionalism had come to be seen, as Edna Heatherington has observed, a backward, "conservative style." Modernists condemned regionalism, Heatherington wrote in her 1978 thesis, "as ignorant, sterile, untruthful—in fact, immoral." [12] Endless jokes were made about tract houses with cosmetic vigas, the state being up to its eyeballs in brown stucco, and about fake lumps in the cement block walls. Modernists saw regional architecture—even the austere mastery of Meem's best work at UNM—to be a form of stage designing. Regional buildings were looked upon as cartoons, as caricatures of real buildings, as skin-deep fakes.

It wouldn't be until the early 1970s, when the new building program at UNM was in high gear, that the fatuousness of the grudge match between modernism and regionalism would become evident. Though the war continued to sputter along on intellectual battlefields, at UNM an unexpected hybrid vigor was becoming manifest in the new buildings. Modernism and regionalism were giving way to one another to create a campus that was at once an architectural laboratory for contextual modernism, for modern buildings appropriate to the New Mexico cultural milieu, and a parklike, pedestrian environment in the middle of dissonant, car-town Duke City.

Regional and modern buildings at UNM entered into a surprising kind of architectural symbiosis. Despite the conflict between the two philosophies, the groundwork for this union was inherent in Meem's respect for the "fundamental form" of our times, and in the purist sentiment that underlies modernist taste. Hodgin Hall, the old Pueblo Revival dormitories, the Alumni Chapel, and most other regional buildings at UNM, all manifest a clarity of line, a gentle massing of shapes, an organic clustering of elegant but unobtrusive forms that arise out of the functional genius of the vernacular building methods from which they are derived. If form follows function—within a cultural context—then Pueblo and Hispanic forms are the very essence of functionality, arising out of the materials of the land to which their cultures had adapted, producing efficient, simple buildings that not only worked, but, of necessity, honestly expressed their structure. This is the kind of building to which modernism wanted to return. Coming as a reaction against buildings that symbolically reinforced a sense of decadent aristocracy in Europe, modernist architecture wanted to get back to the basics. And New Mexico regionalism is as basic as it gets.

One can see the odd parallels between European modernism in the 1920s and Pueblo Revival–style architecture in New Mexico before World War I, by comparing two historically unrelated structures—the now-demolished Central Heating Plant at UNM, completed in 1906, and a 1923 model of the villa project for the Venice Lido by German architect Adolf Loos—that look so much alike as to appear mutually derivative. It seems beyond the realm of possibility, of course, that Adolf Loos was influenced by Edward Cristy, though Loos did spend time in the United States. And although Cristy might have had some contact with protomodernist sentiments in Europe before the war, he certainly was not a pioneering American modernist constructing standardized buildings disguised as Pueblo house blocks. Loos was a great polemicist and theoretician. His purist philosophy influenced Le Corbusier, and his detestation of ornament as an immoral waste of time, effort, and building materials helped to set the tone for architecture well into the twentieth century. Loos believed, high handedly, that "peasant architecture" was an expression of innate culture and being, much as a thorn was an innate expression of a thorny plant. He might well have thought that Pueblo and Hispanic architecture were similarly innate.

The visual relationship between the vanished heating plant and the model villa is uncanny. They look as if they were designed almost in the same place and at the same time. And they foreshadow the present juxtaposition of building forms at UNM. Both are angular, harsh, geometric, modular, with stepped walls, and a complete absence of sculptural ornament, although the heating plant did have some rounded buttresses which seemed ornamental but probably were not. If the Lido villa were colored adobe brown it would fit in as perfectly on the campus in 1988 as it would have on the campus of 1910. Perhaps the early controversies around the Pueblo Revival style had subliminally as much to do with the hard, geometric forms as they did with its implied primitiveness in an age of progress. The turn-of-the-century dislike for such buildings in New Mexico may have been a foreshadowing of the disenchantment with hard-edged, antihistorical modernism in the 1980s.

The New Mexico skyline at UNM—that view from the old Biology Building that takes in the Fine Arts Complex, the bookstore and Woodward Lecture Hall, Ortega Hall, the Humanities Building, and the tower at Zimmerman Library —is a monument to the two prevailing spirits of our times. It embodies both the spirit of international scientific rationalism, which can be faithfully reproduced anywhere on the planet, and the spirit of eccentric locality, irreplaceable and irrevocably tied to a specific cultural and geographic site. If buildings "embody ideas,"[13] then the campus skyline expresses the unstated philosophy here that even the purities of modernism must submit themselves to the gritty and idiosyncratic fascinations of New Mexico.

Some critics have insinuated from time to time that the only thing that holds UNM campus architecture together is the color brown. They hate the color—alluding to it as if it were a kind of dirty rouge, a harloty cosmetic sprayed over the cloth-coat gray of honest concrete. For them, brown is a symbol of decadence, of an odious quaintness reeking with tourists and trashy commercialism, rather than a respectful symbol of the land and the built forms that have been sculpted from it. It is true, of course, that the buildings are brown— shades of buckskin, of tan and clay, or sandy loam. But it is more than color that makes the UNM skyline New Mexican. It is the shapes the color takes.

The Humanities Building by W. C. Kruger and Associates is a modernist massing of horizontal and vertical rectangles and squares. It could as well be a modular, Moshe Safdie, Habitat-type building as it could be a cubist abstraction of Taos Pueblo or the Hopi village of Walpi. Its hard-edged geometry makes it a direct heir of early Pueblo Revival–style buildings at the turn of the century. The massive, fortresslike clustering of Ortega Hall is also heir to revivalist insights. Designed by George Pearl, and frequently maligned for a cement slab skirt creating a dark tunnel around the building, which was not in the architect's original design, Ortega Hall combines the modular clustering of Pueblo forms, with their stepped views of the horizon, with the defensive quality of Hispanic buildings. Faculty office space in Ortega Hall is built around a skylighted interior atrium lounge, which serves the building, much like a hacienda's placita, as a common and protected open space. Though both these buildings, and the others in the campus skyline, are modernist structures, without regional ornament and with no direct symbolic allusions other than their color, all convey a perfect sense of place.

The summit of the skyline is the tower of John Gaw Meem's Zimmerman Library with its five vertical window grooves, in which four levels of windows are recessed, subtly resembling defensive grill work. The tower itself has the quality of a stack of pueblo room blocks, or perhaps what a reconquest Hispanic torreón, a defensive stone or adobe tower, must have seemed like. Although without an exact vernacular model, the tower's sloping form reads as a regional expression, as its clean lines read just as clearly as a modernist gesture. In writing on the impact of modernism in New Mexico, Chris Wilson elaborates on Eleil Saarinen's influence on Meem, quoting from a lecture Saarinen gave at the 1931 AIA Convention in San Antonio, which Meem attended. "Saarinen asked rhetorically," Wilson writes, " 'Can't we take the forms of our forefathers and mold them so that they fit our time and then develop our architecture through tradition?' " [14] With the tower at Zimmerman Library, Meem answers the question with a firm and imposing yes.

Among the most successful other modernist homages to New Mexico land and culture in Albuquerque are George Pearl's addition to Zimmerman Library and his renovation of the reservoir on campus, Antoine Predock's Albuquerque Museum, and Harvey Hoshour's Indian Pueblo Cultural Center.

Pearl's addition to Zimmerman Library is a fine expression of a modernist's sensitivity to context. Assigned by University Architect Van Dorn Hooker the task of making major additions to perhaps the most important building in the city, Pearl designed the eastern expansion of the library with a sense of monumentality that is consistent with both ancient and contemporary building methods. The great sweeping south wall of the addition, bordering on the campus's central plaza across from the Humanities Building, has the feel of what three-story masonry walls at Chaco Canyon or the adobe sides of major churches must have seemed like to passers-by. Curving out and skyward, these wall forms give the feeling of being raised out of the earth, pulled by human art from the body of the land. The southern wall at Zimmerman, which disguises a massive, multistory air conditioning system, evokes in the viewer the sensation of being in the presence of a union between nature and human nature, in which human dwellings resemble the plastic shapes of land forms. In an article about Van Dorn Hooker in his role as major client at UNM for New Mexico architects, Pearl wrote that

at least a decade before "postmodernism" became a popular expression, a great number of architects were steered by Van Dorn Hooker into transcending the philosophy of the international school without abandoning anything except the school's dogmas of placelessness and arrogant ignorance of surroundings.

As a modernist, Pearl continued

Even when we were still striving, elsewhere, to achieve smooth-surfaced cubes sitting in splendid isolation on their militantly unadorned plazas, we overcame ourselves at UNM and produced buildings which lent themselves to fit their place.[15]

One of the strongest works of architecture at UNM is not really a building, yet it is a grand testament to sense of place.

When George Pearl renovated the city reservoir on campus—
an old engineering eyesore that had defied being puebloized,
or modernized for that matter—he went directly to the spirit
of the land. The cap of the reservoir is a sturdy, brown, nuevo
UNM, hard-edge solution to a difficult problem. But around
the cap, on all four sides, is a sloping hillside covered with
thousands of boulder-sized river stones. Gathered from the
San Juan River in the heart of Anasazi country, the beautiful,
rounded, water-polished stones are for me an ultimate linkage
between the necessities of nature, in which nothing is super-
fluous, and the motive to be as good as nature that is inherent
in the best work of modernist and regional architects alike.

The fusion of natural and vernacular forms with modernist
principles is the great success of the UNM campus. If vernacular forms arose both from the necessity of materials and
in homage to land forms, and if regional revival styles echo
the vernacular, then the structural purity and honest necessity
of modernism in a New Mexico context comes full circle.
It absorbs into itself the perfect naturalness of early builders,
who worked with basic geometric forms, and proves John
Gaw Meem's point and more. Not only are ancient forms
modern, but modern forms are ancient too.

The spirit of architectural hybrid vigor at UNM appears
from time to time in significant contemporary buildings in
other parts of town. Near Interstate 40 a mile or so east of Old
Town, Miesian architect Harvey Hoshour designed a stun-
ning modernist building for the Indian Pueblo Cultural Center. The Hoshour building is a minimalist masterpiece, designed in the D shape of Pueblo Bonito, stripped bare of any
ornament or symbolic allusion other than the iconographic
geometry of the major Chacoan metropolis. Although the
Pueblo Cultural Center has been altered by subsequent de-

signers, the clarity of Hoshour's building is still evident. In the same way that Egyptian architect Hassan Fathy distilled the cultural essence of Arabic domes and arches for the design of culturally supportive housing for the poor in Cairo, Hoshour distilled the three-dimensional essence of Pueblo Bonito so it could symbolize not only the ancestry of modern Pueblo Indians, but also the protective, cavelike secrecy of Pueblo society.

In Old Town itself, Antoine Predock's Albuquerque Museum is a strong realization of Pueblo Revival and modernist possibilities. A contextual tour de force, the museum is a massive structure that is delicately low-profiled and appropriate to Old Town's intimate scale. The building defers to Old Town, opens onto it with passageways through tiny, back street shopping plazas, and complements its eclectic array of historic buildings with its own passive solar and site specific design. Like the Pueblo Cultural Center, the museum is without regional ornament or direct allusions to ancient buildings. And it still has the same sense of New Mexico that the best modernist structures at UNM possess. In a way similar to many pueblos, views from the building's windows, alcoves, and patios seem to incorporate parts of the landscape—in this case, views of the Sandia Mountains—into the building itself. For its great size and cultural importance, the museum's form is also remarkably humble. So apparently concerned were the architect and the museum's leadership with being a respectful neighbor to Old Town that they created a massive, high-ceilinged exhibition space, partially below grade, to preserve the building's self-effacing demeanor.

The museum, built in 1979, is a milestone in Albuquerque architecture. The first solar museum in the country, it is also probably the last major institutional building in the city to reflect a regional and modernist aesthetic without drifting over into postmodern metaphor. Its pioneering technology and contextual sensitivity make it a fitting structure in which to explain the city's heritage, so much of which has been concerned with a passion for architecture.

5

A City of Open Spaces

ALTHOUGH the regional and modernist architecture of the University of New Mexico campus makes a compelling statement about the complexity of Albuquerque's urban character, architecture itself has not played a major role in establishing and maintaining the city's sense of place. That has been left to Albuquerque's natural landscape and open spaces. Albuquerque's identity depends more on landscape preservation than architecture because national design trends in commercial and residential development have, since the late nineteenth century, overwhelmed the city's indigenous architectural character.

Albuquerque's leadership didn't choose landscape preservation as a quality-of-life and marketing strategy. Open-space advocacy was first a matter of aesthetics and environmental consciousness. But as the city grew through the 1980s, it became evident that publicly protected land forms and open space were the most visible reminders of Albuquerque's individuality. The foothills of the Sandias and the mountains themselves, the West Mesa volcanoes, the basaltic escarpment below them, the Rio Grande and its bosque woodlands, the old ditch system and arroyos are Albuquerque's bulwarks against sprawling overurbanization and the cultural anonymity that it produces.

In the late 1960s, environmental activists, civic leaders, and enlightened politicians and planners in Albuquerque began to hold views about the land that went counter to the city's traditional development perspective. They understood that cities are not just "built environments." They are natural environments as well, ecosystems and terrains that can be respected or abused by human building. They took to heart what revolutionary ecologists such as Ian McHarge were proposing, "that certain lands are unsuitable for urbanization and others are intrinsically suitable."[1] Before the 1960s, such a thought would have been considered not only grossly impractical but also a potential infringement of personal property rights. By the mid 1980s, however, Albuquerque landscape designer and lexicographer Baker Morrow would define open space as a "landscape design concept" in which a "relatively clear or forested area [is] left untouched in or near a city." Open space, Morrow affirmed, "unsullied by the stigma of a formally assigned function, is necessary for the physical and mental health of city-dwelling human beings."[2]

As of 1989, Albuquerque owned or sustained a controlling interest in 21, 285 acres of open space.[3] That's the fifth largest holding of urban open space in the nation. Albuquerque's open-space program was a deciding factor in *Newsweek* magazine's selecting Albuquerque as one of America's "most livable cities" in 1989,[4] thus countering in a small way the reams of bad publicity the city has received. Albuquerque's respect for its topographical and ecological diversity deserves such recognition. Most cities in the western United States—and many parts of Albuquerque too—deface their natural settings, subduing the landscape with the indifference of conquerers. Such cities are the products of politicians and entrepreneurs who think of the land as an expendable resource. For them, the built environment must replace the natural one. Turning land into gold is the economic fulfillment of Manifest Destiny. In this respect, Albuquerque has always been a typical Western city. Much of its urban form is radically at odds with its natural context. But the undeniable aesthetic power of the mountains, river, and volcanoes—and the farsighted effort to preserve them—mitigates the oppressive influence of the strip-developed wastelands of the city.

My wife and I experienced the saving grace of the land with particular intensity one January night by the Rio Grande, listening to the potent silence of the river flow through the bosque's deep winter calm. It was nearing midnight. Albuquerque was snowbound. We couldn't hear a sound through the maze of ice and trees. The only reminder we had of the city was the opalescence of the sky, from streetlights diffusing through the clouds of snow. It was as if we had awakened to find ourselves in the wilderness, isolated from the twentieth century, surrounded by the mysterious peace of the woods. And yet, of course, we had walked to the river from our car, parked a quarter of a mile away at the Rio Grande Nature Center. We were in the city, not far from residential streets, a half mile across the river from Coors Road, the West Mesa's busiest highway.

Our walk that night through the bosque, on the Nature Center's paved bike trails, was an urban adventure in the wildland of New Mexico. We were safe in the blizzard, protected by the city, yet able to feel the free pulse of the river in a way that New Yorkers, Romans, or Parisians never could with their urban waterways. The Rio Grande through Albuquerque is neither an open sewer nor an aquatic highway. Though tamed by levees, it still has a life of its own. The city hasn't swallowed it. In fact, the woodlands of the river have become part of Albuquerque's urban experience.

One of the most extraordinary vistas in the city embraces a number of Albuquerque's open-space achievements. Looking north from the I-25 Isleta Bridge in the South Valley, through the channel of the Rio Grande, one can see three cones of the West Mesa volcanoes framed between the lush serenity of the bosque's cottonwood forest. You couldn't find a better symbol for Albuquerque at its best, or a more beautiful sight. There, in one view, is a monument to enlightened public policy. The volcanoes and the bosque are the cornerstones of the open-space program that began effectively in 1969.

That year, the City/County Goals Commission—a remarkable and farsighted group composed of a cross-section of the city's leadership and activist communities—"proposed that the unique natural features of the Metropolitan Area be preserved 'by achieving a pattern of development and open space respecting the river land, mesas, mountains, volcanoes, and arroyos.' "[5] In 1971, the city made its first purchases of the West Mesa volcanoes. Two years later, major purchases of open space in the Sandia foothills were made, and a nondevelopment demarcation line for building in the foothills was established anywhere that the slope reached ten percent. By 1975, the City/County Comprehensive Plan was approved, with a third of it devoted to open space. It took another eight years before the Rio Grande Valley State Park—which protects twenty-five miles and six thousand acres of the bosque—was created by the legislature in 1983. And major open-space acquisitions have continued into the present.

The existence of Albuquerque's environmental alter ego might come as a surprise to most casual observers. How could a city that seems to encourage sprawling development of the most heedless kind be concerned about open space? But, indeed, both a history of unrestrained development on virtually any terrain and an ardor for landscape preservation exist side by side in Albuquerque. Such a contradictory view of nature is another symptom of the city's fragmented and confusing urban soul. A closer look at the events of 1969 will help to bring the frustrations arising from this contradiction into focus.

By 1969, Albuquerque had already spread to the mountains, and promoters of huge Levittown-like subdivisions were already grading dirt roads over much of the West Mesa's fragile, hillside, grass terrain. But that year saw major environmental triumphs beyond the Goals Commission's call for an open-space network. Citizen activists and enlightened politicians rose to the occasion to counter a proposal made by the federal Bureau of Reclamation to carry out a program of deforestation along the river, which would eradicate the irreplaceable cottonwood bosque, ostensibly to save water. Alarmed by the insensitivity of such an idea, environmentalists created for the legislature a feasibility study for a Rio Grande Valley State Park. Fourteen years later, the idea was approved by the legislature. Later in 1969, environmentalism in Albuquerque came of age when it rallied opposition to a potentially lucrative but polluting new industry. The Chamber of Commerce voted two to one against the proposed construction of a $62 million paper mill in the Rio Grande Valley between Albuquerque and Santa Fe. And the Albuquerque Citizens Committee—a powerful political group—backed the Chamber by a vote of twenty-one to one in rejecting the mill, owned by Parsons and Whittemore Paper Company of New Jersey. Both groups expressed fears of water and air pollution.[6]

Not only were major environmental issues brought to a

head in 1969, but that year La Luz, an award-winning modern cluster development, opened its doors on the West Mesa. Developed by Ray Graham III and Didier Raven, and designed by Antoine Predock, La Luz works in harmony with the architectural heritage of the region and is both pragmatically and spiritually respectful of the land. Built of adobe, in the middle of forty-four acres held in common by its residents, the La Luz townhouses are surrounded by open space that runs from Coors Boulevard to the bosque. It was a revolutionary idea for its time, preserving land and wildlife habitats without sacrificing profits. At the same time La Luz was making its gesture to the conservation ethic of the future, its philosophical opposite was springing up in the Northeast Heights—the largest apartment complex ever built in the city. Developed by Kassuba Realty Corporation of Palm Beach, Florida, the project contained 1,500 apartments on 117 acres on Montgomery Boulevard between Carlisle and San Mateo.[7] It had the effect of creating out of nothing a whole new district of the city. In comparison, La Luz was an oasis of ecological gentility. But while the concept of cluster development is economically viable for those with modest incomes as well as for the gentry, La Luz remains today an inspiring anomaly, praised but rarely followed. The old Kassuba Project, on the other hand, was the catalyst for massive apartment developments on Montgomery from San Mateo to the mountains. Moderate-density cluster development would have served the same economic and residential purposes without having destroyed the natural landscape.

Albuquerque's open-space movement—as well as the city's overall sense of place—was also heir to a bit of good fortune in 1969. The same Chamber of Commerce that had rejected the Parson and Whittemore paper mill invited Walt Disney Productions to build a gigantic $30 million winter recreation complex at Sandia Peak instead of in Mineral King Valley in California's Sierra Nevada Mountains, where the Sierra Club and other conservationists had been opposing the plan in the courts.[8] Disney considered Albuquerque's offer, but decided the weather on the Sandias was too turbulent for its purposes.[9]

The events of 1969 were on the minds of the Albuquerque leadership community when its business and environmental factions came together to create a comprehensive plan for the city. The plan struggled to integrate Albuquerque's wilderness, urban, and rural environments into a unified vision of the metropolitan complex. The 1988 revision of the plan, drafted in an economic slump and without the catalyst of a national environmental movement, still retains the original emphasis on preserving Albuquerque's unique diversity of life-styles and land-use patterns. It also has strong provisions for what's come to be called "heritage conservation," protecting the city's remaining historic buildings and the vast archaeological treasures still in the ground.

But despite the plan's good intentions, the conflict between what ecologist Gregory Bateson might have called the animate and the inanimate views of planning is intense in Albuquerque.[10] Animate planning treats the environment as a living thing, an organic whole composed of interrelationships, which must be dealt with sensitively through understanding the variety of its differences and internal distinctions. Inanimate planning treats the living environment as a dead thing, a carcass to be rendered into profits. The dead land is to be understood and manipulated not through subtleties of difference, but by the statistical pounding of forces and impacts. It's the conflict between what landscape architect Ian McHarge called designing with nature and what might be called engineering against nature. In the 1950s and

early 1960s, developers in Albuquerque were permitted by
the zoning code to build houses in arroyos and on unprotected
flood plains, perhaps the most unstable and violent micro-
environments in a desert landscape. When it rains, arroyos
channel mountain and foothill runoff to the river. They're
among the most obvious features of the living landscape. In
strong rains, dry arroyos can become destructive walls of
water in a matter of minutes. It's preposterous to build anything in them. But when you perceive the land as a dead
thing, such stupidities can happen—with tragic effect. During a particularly heavy rain in the summer of 1988, for instance, houses near the foothills that were built on, or too
close to, arroyos were heavily damaged by mud. And some
streets, which had been blindly imposed upon the landscape,
acted as arroyos themselves. In a fierce downpour that lasted
no longer than an hour, one young woman was swept out of
her car and drowned on such a street.

Failing to design with nature can cause a sorrowful waste of
resources as well. It wasn't until the mid 1970s, for instance,
that city government required Albuquerque's innumerable
parking lots to be planted with trees and designed to conserve
rainfall by channeling runoff into tree beds and sinks for other
vegetation. The result of the parking-lot planting ordinance
is the transformation of many parts of Albuquerque's commercial landscape from moonscapes of asphalt to appealing
urban copses. The gigantic parking lot at Coronado Center,
the city's largest shopping mall, has become a sort of bosque
in itself, a visual oasis on one of the city's hottest and busiest
commercial strips.

In 1990, the city was still battling over wasteful residential development on and around the West Mesa's volcanic escarpment, site of the nation's best collection of prehistoric
Native American rock art and the new seventeen-mile-long

Petroglyph National Monument. Developers since the 1960s had been given the go-ahead to treat the distinctive geologic forms of the escarpment as if they didn't exist, subdividing the salable land so that sometimes half a home site would be draped over a high precipice of volcanic rock. The developers' idea, with the tacit permission of the zoning code, was to simply blast away the rock, and the rock art with it.

But the economic impulse to treat the topography as an erasable impediment has been, indeed, countered to some degree. Although the tension will probably never ease between conservation and development interests, the popular movement to create an environmentally sensitive comprehensive plan has become a part of the enduring official policy of city government. And in the age of the greenhouse effect and global urban competition, the lessons of Albuquerque's environmental history could prove indispensable.

What is it about the landscape of New Mexico, and the middle Rio Grande Valley, that inspires otherwise politically dormant citizens to come to its defense? What makes so many people look at the land not so much as a financial asset but as a spiritual necessity? Why is the land so personal to so many?

One answer comes from Albuquerque landscape painter Wilson Hurley. "There are very few people who have access to this kind of beauty within five miles of their homes. It's more—or at least just as—beautiful here as at the Grand Canyon or Canyon de Chelly. It's just not as well advertised." [11] Aesthetically, the Albuquerque area is cast in the image of a high-desert Eden, charged with the pure power of creation, and yet vulnerable to the frailties of its human stewards. One can't help but get emotional about the place, especially if it's threatened. Many people stay in Albuquerque because they cannot imagine living without the sense of freedom that the land instills. It's also true, however, that the central New Mexican landscape around Albuquerque is one of North America's most demanding urban settings. Its aridity and openness, its humbling immensity can be liberating or can drive some people crazy. Albuquerque has always been a tragic leader among cities in suicides per capita.

The Albuquerque oasis is like a miniature Los Angeles Basin, backed on the east by abrupt, weather-altering mountains, and opening to the west not on an ocean of water, but on an oceanic expanse of lava, sand, and rock. The natural splendors of the place are immediately apparent. The landscape that Albuquerque inhabits is a sensual and a spiritual haven, one that's dominated by color, texture, creatures, and inspiring perspectives, not by human plans and goals.

At first glance, the wilderness around Albuquerque is an ascetic color field of browns, blacks, grays, and ochres set off against clouds in the dreamscape blue of the sky and against the river's seasonal, serpentine body of green. Dust, dirt, and mud, though, are what the newcomer first sees. But slowly the power of green becomes apparent. It asserts itself everywhere, in the driest gravel and the coldest mountain crags. It takes the form not just of bottomland cottonwoods and highland pines and aspen, but of Russian olives and salt cedars, tumbleweeds, clover, cattails, willows, wild mustard, nightshade, gourd leaf, rabbit bush, asters, thistles, goatheads, and the seemingly infinite variety of scrubs and grasses that covers the sand hills and alluvial plains of the mountains.

The textures of the land seem as harsh and ascetic as its colors. It's all stickers, prickly weeds, volcanic stone, river rock, and hot, abrasive sand. But if you spend time making adobes, or mud plastering, or poking around anthills (a favorite winter pastime of amateur rock-hounds and geologists), you discover the sand is rich in tiny jewels from the erosion of pre-Cambrian granites that cap the Sandia and Manzano mountains. On anthills, in particular, you'll find granular nuggets of rich jasper, feldspar, translucent quartz, olivine, and pink granite, as well as polished lava, obsidian, and chert from the volcanos. Some people collect garnets from anthills in the North Valley. And once I found the miniscule jaw of a lizard tossed out by the ants on their midden of tiny stones.

That Albuquerque is a city of open spaces one can affirm on a small scale by observing the profusion of desert life in the city itself—the insects, snakes, lizards, roadrunners, spiders, rodents, occasional bears, coyotes, and the unstoppable, concrete-cracking weeds that pay no attention to the built environment. Its open spaces can also be understood on an imaginative scale by looking to the western horizon. Even though the Ceja Mesa west of the river is filling up with subdivisions, the essential character of this New Mexican city is clearly symbolized by the emptiness of the land. The state is almost vacant. With the fifth largest land mass in the nation, New Mexico has just over a million and a half people. South of Albuquerque, for instance, from a little settlement called Los Chavez, one could travel due west and wouldn't hit a human habitation of any size until the Arizona-California border, five hundred miles away. One could probably walk for a month and never see a soul, except when crossing highways.

The eyeline west from Los Chavez is a perfect metaphor for Albuquerque's wilderness condition. Looking west, one can get lost from civilization with a simple gaze, emblematic of why living in Albuquerque's open spaces can be such a startling urban experience. In the middle of the fiercest traffic, almost anywhere in town, you can find yourself suddenly looking up, adjusting your focus, and seeing distant mountains coming into perspective and becoming a part of the visual city. The traffic itself can seem for a moment like a mirage. The horizons become the intimate experience. And one remembers that Albuquerque itself is not an eternal given, but a transitory human settlement on the anatomy of the Albuquerque Basin.

If far horizons can become intimate perspectives within the inner reaches of the city, internal open spaces can sometimes push the city so far away that it all but disappears. If one shifts perception from gazing out to focusing in on the wildlands of the river, the city recedes, vanishing in the distance, and you find yourself in the middle of what once was known as the American Nile.

The Middle Rio Grande Valley used to be one of the West's great agricultural heartlands. It fed large populations of Pueblo Indians, and their Spanish conquerers, for centuries. Twenty years after the arrival of the railroad in 1880, Albuquerque was exporting produce as far as California and was famous for orchards, vineyards, and vegetables. And the whole enterprise was built largely on an irrigation system that existed in the valley long before the Spanish arrived. In fact, it's one of the oldest water works in North America. Historian Marc Simmons maintains that the present ditch system was started before the Pueblo Revolt of 1680.[12] Some archaeologists believe that when the Spanish came to the New World with Moorish irrigation techniques, they adapted them to the existing Pueblo canals they found when they first settled the valley in the early seventeenth century.

The acequia environment as we know it today started in 1925. Because Spanish and Indian fields had no drains to carry off excess water, the rich agricultural land of the valley eventually became waterlogged, crippling Albuquerque's farming industry. The Middle Rio Grande Conservancy District was formed in 1925 to drain the swampy land, improve the ditches, and build a levee to diminish disastrous Rio Grande flooding. The Conservancy still administers the acequias today. Running from Cochiti Lake, some thirty miles north of Albuquerque, down through the center of the city, and south to the Bosque del Apache Wildlife Refuge, the ditch network is immense. The Conservancy is responsible for 219 miles of canals and irrigation systems, 55 miles of which are so inaccessible that they have to be maintained by hand labor. In addition, it has 155 miles of river levees and 144 miles of surface and subsurface drains to look after.

Albuquerque's network of ditches, or acequias, are perhaps the city's greatest hidden treasure. Planners and historians think they might be unique as far as North American cities are concerned. In the middle of the car culture of Albuquerque, the acequia system not only irrigates family farms and nurtures rural life-styles, its waters create a lush public garden, complete with walking paths, the length and breadth of the valley. Albuquerque's planning department is hoping the acequia network becomes a formal part of a citywide open-space environment that would link up with Sandia Mountain hiking trails, city-owned West Mesa open space, the arroyo network, the Rio Grande State Park, and city open space in the Sandia foothills. In the North Valley, the acequia network already forms a spiritual and environmental link with the Rio Grande Nature Center State Park, which contains a building that is, in many ways, an embodiment of the city's progressive spirit.

Like La Luz, the Nature Center building was designed by Antoine Predock. Completed in 1982 on 170 acres of wetlands in the forests of the Rio Grande not five miles from downtown, the Nature Center is the epitome of adaptive architecture guided by an ecological aesthetic. It is, indeed, a building designed *with* nature. Almost invisible, it acts as a blind within which visitors can unobtrusively observe a wild life habitat that would otherwise be disrupted by their physical presence. The building's public face is a low-lying hill in a cottonwood grove with a corrugated culvert protruding from it, inviting investigation and adventure. The culvert is the entrance to the building, and channels one's attention in the same way it would collect and guide water. Coming through the secret passageway of the culvert, one enters a room that carries the feeling of a diving bell with viewing ports that frame scenes of the nature preserve outside. The building is a sort of architectural telescope/microscope that focuses contemplation. Yet it also serves as part of a dam that creates and encloses a large ponding area for water fowl.

The nature preserve itself is located on land known as Candelaria Farms, about a quarter of a mile west of Rio Grande Boulevard. Owned in pieces by the city, the state, and the Conservancy District, the preserve is bordered on the west by the river and on the east by the Duranes Lateral, an irrigation ditch that is one of the city's most beautiful walking environments. The preserve, with its marsh, ponds, discreet Nature Center, and irrigated fields used for feed, attracts migrating birds and permits local plant and animal species to flourish.

It is not possible for people to say they really know Albuquerque if they haven't experienced the bosque and its neighboring fields and ditches. Right in the heart of the city, even now with the pressing encroachment of the built environment, one can still see bats, mice, gophers, beaver, coyotes, ground squirrels, muskrats, raccoons, skunks, and rabbits along the ditch banks. One can also find meadowlarks, ducks, ring-necked pheasants, Gambel's quail, killdeer, hawks, owls, cranes, and even gulls, herons, and egrets. There are garter snakes and bull snakes; there are skinks, lizards, and turtles, as well as leopard frogs, bull frogs, Woodhouse's toads, and tiger salamanders.

The ditch system and Nature Center preserve, along with the flood control channeling of the Rio Grande, which created an environment suitable for the germination of the river's huge cottonwood forest, are among Albuquerque's most impressive contemporary "urban" successes. Engineering acumen was combined with ecological and aesthetic sensitivity to create a built environment that is energized and ennobled by the natural landscape it inhabits.

It's Albuquerque's cultural landscape, however, that will most likely be the catalyst that solidifies Albuquerque's urban image in the 1990s. The Petroglyph National Monument on the West Mesa, signed into law by President Bush in June 1990, combines preservation of open space with heritage conservation in a way that gives Albuquerque a unique human landscape running parallel with the river through the middle of the city.

The monument is both a huge expanse of land, with vast holdings in prehistoric Native American rock art, and an immense planning and urban-design problem. It encompasses seventeen miles of the West Mesa volcanic escarpment, with 7,369 acres, and 15,000 to 17,000 petroglyphs, some of them at least 500 years old. And suburban development is already encroaching on the west and east. Although the monument exists on paper, much of the land remained to be acquired when the president signed the monument into law. The petroglyphs for years had been objects of vandalism and outright theft. And planners were worried about how to protect them from mischief as well as from the rapid growth overtaking the west side of the city.

Ike Eastvold, the citizen activist who more than anyone is responsible for the monument's creation, worried that if development near the petroglyphs is out of scale, if it conflicts with the monument "instead of harmonizing with it, the whole integrity of the national monument could be degraded." [13] In 1989, Eastvold told a national open-space conference in Albuquerque that he organized the Friends of the Albuquerque Petroglyphs in 1986 because he was not only amazed by the significance of the petroglyphs themselves, but also dismayed at their degradation. He said homes had been platted on the escarpment, many petroglyphs had been used for target practice, a huge trash heap had formed in an archaeologically sensitive canyon, the city's Public Works Department had drilled a tunnel through the middle of the escarpment, and a major highway was being planned through the area. [14] Despite these problems, in only four years Eastvold and the Friends, with more than 500 members in twenty-eight states and three foreign countries, lobbied successfully with city, state, and national officials to create the monument. It is a remarkable achievement.

Although the National Park Service has two other urban parks—the Golden Gate National Recreation Area in San Francisco, and the Gateway National Recreation Area in New York City—the Petroglyph National Monument is the only urban archaeological site in the national system. It is also unique because the land will be owned and managed in partnership with state and city governments. In 1988, a National Park Service study estimated the monument could draw as many as 400,000 visitors to the city and account for some $1.5 million in revenue. [15] The monument will be the eastern gateway of the National Park Service's Masau Trail, a tour route linking Chaco Canyon, Mesa Verde, Navajo National Monument and other ancient Anasazi sites.

With seven major West Mesa developments in close proximity to the monument, public officials and activists will have to meet taxing political and design challenges to make the most of the monument's cultural and natural resources. They will need to follow Ian McHarge's advice "to ask the land where are the best sites" for specific uses, and convince developers and property owners it's in their interest to do so.[16] As Eastvold says, "Although the national monument brings new constrictions on what you can and can not do on its immediate borders, it also brings some new opportunities and we can end up with a higher quality of life on the West Side."[17] Rex Funk, director of Albuquerque's open-space program, put the problem succinctly: The monument is "a shoestring that runs through a large developed area. . . . We're fighting for all the buffer we can get."[18]

Creating harmony between the monument and residential developments will require putting the powers and sophistication of what cultural geographer J. B. Jackson calls the "political landscape" at the service of the natural one. Jackson maintains that humans, as both political animals and creatures of a habitat, "see the landscape as something shared; they assume that human beings cannot survive and fulfill themselves unless there is a landscape to hold them together in a group."[19] Usually, however, the political landscape prevails over the natural one.

But in the last twenty years, Albuquerque's public genius has brought the two together. As a group, Albuquerque voters have overwhelmingly approved open-space bond issues. They understand, I think, that open-space landscape holds Albuquerque together as a city. Land forms and natural environments give the city's multicultural population common points of reference with which to identify. Preservation of the land unites the city politically. And open space gives citizens a chance to feel a collective sense of pride. As a populist economic-development strategy, open space is anti-elitist. And while it does nothing directly to counter the problems of gentrification, it adds nothing to them. Using the land to help create urban identity is an egalitarian option to the "quaintscape"[20] solutions of cities such as Santa Fe.

6

A Spiritual Region

RECOGNIZING and respecting intangible qualities in urban environments seems an impossible exercise. Yet, I believe, accounting for deep cultural realities is essential to the understanding of a city's identity. What is it that gives a place its soul? It is more than architecture, more than urban form, cultural commodities, and even natural landscapes. It has to do with the inner lives of the people in and around the city—their values and their beliefs. The attraction of Albuquerque, for instance, cannot be explained by its physical presence alone. Even the landscape itself is meaningless until people give it meaning. The power of New Mexico, and Albuquerque's saving grace, is that the state is a spiritual region.

The Pueblo Revolt of 1680, along with the cultural and religious isolation of Spanish settlers in the eighteenth and early nineteenth centuries, established for Albuquerque a spiritual context unique in North America. No other major American city is surrounded by a ring of Native American urban enclaves which, as far as we know, preserve largely intact an indigenous spiritual tradition that is at least 1,500 to 2,000 years old. And intertwined with the mysteries of Pueblo cere-

monialism is the presence of nearly 400 years of New Mexico
Catholicism, a singular expression of Christianity nurtured
in the secluded outback of the far frontier of New Spain and
gaining much of its power from the sixteenth-century ascetic
mysticism of Santa Teresa of Avila and St. John of the Cross.

These are living faiths of great power and endurance. In
a seemingly rootless modern city like Albuquerque, which
is swamped by commercialism and almost constant change,
they are cultural anchors more tenacious and determining
than the land. For contemporary urban nomads who care to
know where they are, Southwesterners who want to inhabit
real places rather than the false fronts of a generic American shopping culture, the presence of Native American and
Hispanic spirituality in Albuquerque has a tremendous, even
life-altering, force.

But how does one assess the impact of spirituality on the
built environment and its inhabitants? Its influence is indirect
at best, though in New Mexico it does form one of the cultural bases of regional revival-style architecture. Buildings
like the Spanish Pueblo–style Zimmerman Library at UNM
or the Pueblo modernism of the Albuquerque Museum evoke
associations with the cultural richness of Hispanic and Native
American religious life. In Pueblo society, religion is said to
permeate all social interactions and cultural products, even
architecture, which is not separate from nature, but seen as
a human extension of the environment.[1] And contemporary
revival styles modeled on native Hispanic architecture are derived from the forms and details of mission churches and
domestic buildings.

But the spiritual context of New Mexico is more than a
matter of architectural imagery, of course. It pervades Albuquerque with a kind of psychic effervescence, which keeps
one feeling slightly off-balance and metaphysically awake. Its

impact on the urban environment, though, can only be assessed intuitively, through personal experience.

The survival of the Pueblo way of life is, for me, a cultural miracle. In the confines of a dominating modern culture such as ours, which devours the past and scatters the fragile patterns of older societies, the persistence of ancient ways of life and, to some extent, of folk religions, is almost unheard of. Yet around Albuquerque are more than twenty pueblo villages, and innumerable archaeological sites of pueblo ancestors. Each village has an indigenous spiritual life of its own, embodying the fundamentals of an earth-centered pan-Pueblo cosmology.[2] In its relation to the past, Albuquerque is much like Rome, Athens, and Mexico City. It is built within an archaeological precinct. It is a modern place rising on the ruins of ancient post-Anasazi cities. It is also, however, utterly different from other ancient sites that have evolved into modern cities. The Pueblo descendants of Albuquerque's dead cities are still alive and practicing their culture with religious intensity.

Pueblo urbanism and its identification with the landscape, along with Hispanic religious architecture and village patterns, set standards and expectations for city building in New Mexico. Albuquerque has a demanding standard to live up to. And, indeed, the comparison is unfair. How can one judge a modern American car town against the cultural genius inherent in village life? But fair or not, the comparison is made subliminally all the time. People who love New Mexico expect Albuquerque to be inspired by the ecological sensitivity of the pueblos and the functional grace of Hispanic towns and churches. And, of course, they are continually disappointed.

And then there's the matter of civic loneliness. Albuquerque, like other Western boomtowns, is largely a city of privacies and private interests. Our public life, and our pub-

lic spaces, are almost nonexistent. The conspicuous presence
of Pueblo cities that not only architecturally reflect the land
around them, but that also work as nurturing cultural con-
tainers which reinforce the spirit of public sharing and commitment, makes the isolation of life in Albuquerque all the
more poignant and difficult to bear.

Commercial Albuquerque often seems like a 1950s Baby-
lon imposed on the austere and ascetic environment of Pueblo
and Hispanic spiritualism. But like the land that gives the
city life and hope, indigenous spirituality energizes Albuquerque's inhabitants; its artifacts become talismans of a mys-
tical connection with the land, and of an inspiring medieval
piety, at once innocent, profoundly wise, and enduring.

For people like myself who become adopted natives of
New Mexico, who stake out their own spiritual homeland
here, the surrounding countryside is filled with architectural
icons that resonate with sincerity, simplicity, and mystery,
such as the kivas of Kuaua and Chaco Canyon, and the ruins
of the church at Quarai.

Part of the Salinas National Monument, south of Albuquerque at the end of the Manzano Mountains, Quarai is a
ruined Catholic mission church, constructed on the site of a
sizable Piro pueblo, and built out of layers of dressed sandstone, which looks to the casual eye not unlike the ruins of
Chaco Canyon. Quarai is where Pueblo and Spanish mysticism merge. Along with the ruined missions at Abo, several
miles to the west, and at Gran Quivira to the South, Quarai
was built by Pueblo labor and designed by Franciscan friars
who had, as far as we know, no formal architectural training.
The Pueblos around the Estancia Valley were first contacted
by the Spanish in the 1580s, but were not converted to Christianity until forty years later. By 1626, Nuestra Señora de la
Purísima Concepción de Cuarac, Quarai's formal name, had

its first resident priest. The church was built almost in the middle of the pueblo, dominating it symbolically and politically. But not fifty years later, Quarai and the other Salinas missions were abandoned, perhaps as many as four years before the Pueblo revolt of 1680. Famine, disease, and Apache raiders are said to have been the cause. When the Spanish reconquered New Mexico, they never reinhabited the missions, perhaps because the Pueblo people themselves had fled the area, joining other villages north and south of Isleta.

At Quarai one feels the miracle of faith and the tragedy of religious conflict with equal power. But it's the sheer, startling beauty of the place that first charges it with significance for Albuquerque. Traveling south down Highway 14, one drives through a number of small Hispanic mountain villages. Each has its own little church and parcels of rolling farmland and pasture. None gives a hint of what is to be found at Quarai. When one reaches the Quarai turnoff and drives west, solitary hawks are often seen gliding on the mountain air currents. But there's nothing much else in sight until you round an inconspicuous corner. And there before you, with no warning, are the towering walls of what looks like the spectre of a cathedral risen spontaneously from the rocky land. With thick sandstone walls that rise in some places sixty feet high, Quarai has the feeling of a Mont-Saint-Michel, an island of architecture, a spiritual fantasy.

Imagine a handful of Franciscan friars, backed up, of course, by at least the threat of Spanish arms, occupying a pueblo of hundreds of people, most deeply suspicious if not intractably hostile to their intrusion. And imagine these friars cajoling and forcing that whole population to build a sandstone-rubble-walled cathedral in the middle of their pueblo, conquering it architecturally with a fortresslike space in which to worship an alien god. These Franciscans must have been men of unconquerable personal self-confidence and religious inner strength. One can still feel the power of their presence in the walls of Quarai.

One cold, winter, moonlit night many years ago, when Quarai was not yet a national monument, that presence took a physical form that terrified me at first, then sent my spirit soaring. A dirt road went to Quarai from the turnoff in those days, and it was slippery with mud and snow becoming slush and ice. But seeing Quarai rising from the land in moonlight was worth the hazard. It was as if we had stumbled across a sepulcher bathed in numinous light. The night was frozen as we walked through the mounded ruins of the old pueblo to the entrance of the church. Inside the roofless building, the sky literally flooded in. We walked through the light, filled with awe and the strange apprehension that comes with the harmony of silence and the majesty of ruins. Cold to the bone, shivering with tension, we approached the apse where the altar once stood. As we thought about the services given from that spot three hundred years ago, we heard a rustle, then a rushing, then a muscular hushing of what sounded like wings. Suddenly, exploding from the niches that once held the roof beams, two snow-white owls filled the moonlight with their bodies. Terrified at first, then overwhelmed, we turned in time to see angelic shadows glide over the snow and off into the darkness of the pueblo ruins and the hills.

The mystery of that moment put the achievement of the friars in perspective. The owls somehow embodied the synthesis of land and stone, of Pueblos and Spanish. Those Franciscans built their churches not only with Pueblo labor, but with Pueblo building techniques, techniques that had made Pueblo peoples, by the end of the first millennium, the greatest architects and city-builders in North America. The friars unknowingly built upon the engineering masterpieces of Chaco Canyon, Mesa Verde, and other Anasazi urban sites. These cities of sandstone, mud, fiber, and timber were the product of a personal and cultural genius every bit as tenacious and unconquerable as that of the friars. That the religious practices of the Pueblos survived the military and missionary zeal of Christian Spain creates an image for us today of modern Albuquerque rising not only from the high mountain desert, but also from the religious and social history of two implacable cultures. For three hundred years, they fought and compromised, and then learned to coexist, not only with each other but with Anglo America. At Quarai, the ruins of the pueblo and the broken body of the church are both embraced by the land in which the past is buried.

To live in contemporary Albuquerque is to live in the presence of that past, and to be a part of the future it has become. But I am convinced that even if there were few physical remains and no metaphoric references to the Pueblo and Hispanic past, one would still feel in Albuquerque the spiritual impact of these cultures. One senses its significance rising from the landscape like a clearness in the air, an intense sensation of home feeling for a place that shouldn't deserve it. Modern Albuquerque seems like a little bubble of materialism in an ocean of ancient faith. Yet that ocean and its remains create the conditions that make the city so much more than its negative reputation.

One has only to visit Kuaua and Chaco Canyon to recognize that presence, or observe the *luminarias* on the graves of a *camposanto,* drive past the Duranes Chapel, attend a dance at Santo Domingo Pueblo, or feel the presence of the mythological powers that the city's treasury of petroglyphs allude to.

Often when I hunt for sightings of petroglyphs along Albuquerque's West Mesa escarpment on the way to visit the ruins of Kuaua, it becomes clear to me that the geography of the middle Rio Grande Valley was once, itself, an icon of spiritual mysteries. Amid the abstract religious symbols—the spirals, mazes, effigies, and kachina figures—of the area's more than 15,000 pieces of Anasazi rock art, one finds here and there realistic landscape representations, such as unmistakable line drawings of the Sandias, depictions of nearby horizons with morning stars rising above them, and even what looks like the meandering course of the Rio Grande. In the religious context of the petroglyphs, these references to the land remind me of portraits of saints or medieval visions of Christ in glory or the Virgin Mary enthroned. And why shouldn't the great sweep of the Sandias be considered an icon of spiritual majesty, of the power and rhythm of the universe as it flows and changes, like breathing, the freedom of water, or the movement of the air? For some Pueblos, that flow "described as *Po-wa-ha* (water-wind-breath), is the essence of life."[3] The valley is charged with centuries of awe. The Sandias, known to the Tewa-speaking Pueblos north of Albuquerque as Oku Pin or Turtle Mountain, is one of the four sacred mountains of the northern Pueblos. Alfonso Ortiz, in *The Tewa World*, says that the Sandias, along with the other mountains, are "endowed with sacredness in several ways," including having an earth navel, or *nan sipu,* in which a guardian deity resides.[4] For many natives of the city, and many who have migrated to Albuquerque and now call it home, the Sandias themselves have been a guardian presence, at once protecting and symbolizing the sanctuary that the city and its natural environment provide.

Arriving at the ruins of Kuaua, where perhaps Pueblo peoples first encountered the Spanish, one is in the presence of a human place built at the foot of cathedral mountains. Kuaua was a Pueblo town, perhaps reminiscent of Isleta or Sandia Pueblo today. But in ruins, it has the feeling of a cloister, similar in outward form to parts of Christian Quarai, although made of puddled mud, not stone. The major difference between the two, however, is that Kuaua is not dominated by the ruins of a church. Its packed urban precinct is designed around inner plazas and underground religious structures known as kivas. Plazas and kivas are places of both interaction and celebration, places in which private meditation and social communion combine. The ground plan of the city of Kuaua is an artifact of spiritual integration, of a way of daily life in which purely secular concerns do not exist. In that sense, Kuaua and many contemporary pueblos do seem like cloisters, holy places in which the social opportunity for living good Pueblo lives is constantly provided for.

No outsider can hope to understand the moral cosmologies of Pueblo cultures. But the European imagination has read into Pueblo ceremonialism a deep relationship with the land, though not a mastery over it. And ethnographic data seem to confirm this interpretation. So it's no surprise that Kuaua, for instance, should have a special relationship to the Sandias and the Rio Grande. It's as if the community had placed itself in proximity to sacred objects, as a parishioner might pray at the foot of a saint. Everyone who visits Kuaua at Coronado State Park and picnics by the river is struck by the splendor of the place. And I'm sure it was the same for the Tiwas of Kuaua. For me, the soaring of the mountains and the river's ancient path combine to make the site a talisman of spiritual energy and elation.

The landscape of Kuaua becomes a sacred precinct, one that is matched in my imagination only by the ascetic clarity of Chaco Canyon. In the same way that the mountains and river drew the Tiwa, the religious power infused through Chacra Mesa and its canyon must have been an undeniable attraction to the Anasazi. Chaco is an oceanic place in which the past and future converge in the stratigraphy of the land forms, the delicate horizontal masonry of the ruins, and the time-lapsing fluidity of the sky. Few places on earth have such a potent spiritual gravity about them. To a romantic outsider like myself, one who is not only alien to their culture but also alienated by time, it makes intuitive sense to surmise that the Anasazi felt physically connected to the canyon in a way that a mere visitor never could. They lived there for more than three hundred years, and seemed to bond to the place in a way that can be explained only through the metaphor of their architecture. As Vincent Scully has said in his book on Pueblo architecture, *Pueblo: Mountain, Village, Dance*, ancient civilizations tend to imitate natural forms in their buildings and include landmarks as part of their urban design.[5] Taos Mountain, for instance, is considered a northern boundary of Taos Pueblo. And at Sandia and Santa Ana pueblos, the Sandia Mountains are considered the eastern edge of their main plazas.[6] At Chaco, the bond between the Anasazi and the spirit of the canyon is seen in the stratographic layering of their masonry, which mirrors the sedimentary deposits that make up the canyon walls. Such Chacoan masonry veneers appear to have no functional or aesthetic use. The intricate horizontal layering was covered over with mud plaster on the exterior walls, and with mud and whitewash inside the rooms. I don't think it's far-fetched to say that the Chaco people were simply content to know that beneath the plaster their walls were homages to the canyon itself, reflecting not only its form, but their deep and affectionate attachment to it. It is as if the canyon had given itself to them, as if they had joined with it, had made it their habitat by adding themselves and their imagination to it through the tangible rock forms of their buildings. Such hidden symbolism is not unique. Spanish adobe makers, for instance, were known to place images of the cross in the middle of their bricks. The image would never be seen, but the builder would know it was there.

It's conceivable to me as well that the great **D** shape of Pueblo Bonito mirrors the curving backs of caves in which other and perhaps earlier Anasazis built their villages. The sandstone caves of Tsegi Canyon, Canyon de Chelly, and Mesa Verde were probably occupied by Basketmakers well before the crystalization of Anasazi culture. The **D** shape, and the modified **E** form of other Chacoan sites, may have been designed in homage to the generous shelter of the land, reflecting not only ancestral memory but the value that conservative Chacoan builders placed on demonstrations of gratitude and respect. The circle form of the kiva, however, seems to relate less directly to specific sites. Holes dug in the ground are round until given another form. Fire depressions, pits for storing grain, eroded sandstone cisterns are all circular shapes, as are navels, dust devils, ant lion traps, and reeds. By mirroring the shape of sun, moon, navels, pupils, and the natural roundness of the holes made by digging sticks in which corn is planted, the round Anasazi kiva connects within itself a symbol of unification, of a common identity among humans, animals, plants, earth, wind, and the heavens.

The land itself makes no discrimination between Christians and Pueblos. The rock walls of Quarai, which look so much like the rougher masonry of late Chaco ruins, are formed into the shape of a cross, not that of a **D**, **E**, or **O**. And not only can the land be shaped into symbols, it is also where we plant our dead. Grave sites become settlements of the dead, both communities and shrines, or, as in many European and New World cities, miniature golf-course versions of Eden.

But the spiritual atmosphere of the Albuquerque region is not funereal or otherworldly. It is of this world. Few mass burial sites, for instance, have been found associated with Anasazi ruins. But when skeletal remains have been found, they've frequently been under the floors of living quarters. And kachina spirits, who visit Hopi pueblos on an annual cycle, are spoken of as dead relatives. The deceased are not banished but are spiritually contained within the community of the living. Just as a widower might still feel married to his late wife, so the living maintain an emotional and ritual connection with their dead.

This sense of community also can be felt in the presence of Hispanic graveyards, *camposantos* or holy grounds, in and around Albuquerque. One of the most beautiful and flourishing *camposantos* is on the corner of Edith Boulevard and Odelia, on the northern edge of Santa Barbara/Martínez-town, venerable barrios that grew up east of the tracks after the coming of the railroad in 1880. The community graveyard, named Santa Barbara after a martyred girl killed by her father for being a Christian, is dry and dusty compared to the more luxuriant modern cemeteries to the north—Sunset Memorial Park, and Mount Calvary, where many of Albuquerque's old Italian families are interred. These cemeteries, with their pastoral rolling lawns and suburban groves and avenues of shade trees, are not used by a particular community; the whole town uses them. But the *camposanto* of Santa Barbara belongs to the neighborhood, is an extension of it, a spiritual extension that gives its hardscrabble landscape an immediate visual sensation of the deepest and most constant faith.

As an artifact of the built environment, the Santa Barbara *camposanto* retains its natural setting. It contrasts sharply with the manicured island of pink California-Spanish townhouses called Sun Village just east up the hill, or its modernistic neighbor, the bunkerlike new Albuquerque High School called Bulldog City. The *camposanto*'s uncovered landscape is that of the steep incline of the stony East Mesa sand hills as they rise from the flood plain of the Rio Grande. There's nothing paradisal about this hard and elemental environment. It's a place of communion shorn of suburban metaphors and allusions. It belongs to the ground it inhabits. Its profusion of tombstones, monuments, and crosses, normally free of weeds and glowing with bouquets of real and artificial flowers, is clearly an undisguised part of the neighborhood which is also built on the sand hills. If the residents of Santa Barbara/Martíneztown suddenly became wealthy, I don't know if they'd roll out sod among the grave furniture of the *camposanto*. From my perspective, money doesn't seem to have much to do with it. The place is what it is; its form has a clarity and power very much like the numinous presence of the mountain. The harsh though vulnerable matter–of–factness of the place conveys an un–self–conscious intensity of emotion that even a motorist can feel while driving past into the consumer suburbs of the Heights. A similar illumination of emotion can be felt on Christmas and New Year's Eve, when the visual isolation of the *camposanto* from its grassy neighbors is healed. All three cemeteries are joined those nights in celebration by a star field of *luminarias*. The night sky is symbolically spread out across the graves in a profusion of candlelight glowing from thousands of brown paper bags. *Luminarias* usually decorate the homes of the living. But on such nights the living and the dead, the heavens and the earth, belong to a common territory of human light. Overlooking the graveyards from the interstate, one senses a sharing of homecoming and emotional reunion.

West of Santa Barbara/Martíneztown, near Old Town, is the community of Los Duranes with its beautiful little church restored by area residents in the mid 1980s. It, too, is a monument to hope and renewal. As Susan Dewitt writes in her book *Historic Albuquerque Today*, Duranes has remained "a small, semi-agricultural and fairly poor district, in comparison with other North Valley communities." In spite of this, "Duranes is a very cohesive neighborhood of mostly long-term residents. . . . Like other communities of the valley, it keeps the pattern of fields and farms and small gardens, ditches, wandering dirt roads, the sense and feel of country in the midst of the city."[7] The Duranes Chapel is two blocks west of Rio Grande Boulevard on Indian School Road. The square adobe chapel still has its wooden steeple and is considered the center of the neighborhood, even though, Dewitt writes, the village church is now located in nearby Los Luceros. Driving past the Duranes Chapel, one senses a pattern of life and faith that thrives in the protection of that private and straightforward building.

It is possible to experience that same sense of spiritual and communal intensity when witnessing Pueblo ceremonials. And such encounters can change your life. A good many New Mexicans use Albuquerque as a base for pilgrimages into the landscape of Anasazi and Pueblo culture. It's safe to say that no other city dwellers in North America—other than those in the metropolitan tourist village of Santa Fe—can get into their cars and in less than an hour cross barriers of time and culture to arrive at urban environments that are rooted a thousand years into their own living history. This is not to say that Pueblo cities are somehow frozen in the past, or that the cultures they contain and defend are throwbacks, living specimens of a dead past. Pueblo culture has always been self-confident and resilient enough to adapt to traumatic changes in its political environment without losing its fundamental identity. Santo Domingo Pueblo, for instance, is among the most conservative and withdrawn of all Rio Grande pueblos.

Yet the wildly satirical and often frightening sacred humor carried on by members of clown associations, which punctuates public dances at the pueblo, is full of modern jokes and allusions directed at non-Indian politics and societies. Walking into the long dance plaza of Santo Domingo during a ceremonial and coming upon the entire city meditating together, laughing together, believing in one another, is miraculous itself. Even if the ceremonies are largely unintelligible to outsiders, they still convey, if not content, then conviction and reality. And, of course, our personal interpretations of what we experience are as inaccessible to the Santo Domingans as their mysteries are to us. But we can all share the humor.

Each of us has our own history of such moments. Mine includes the first tablita, or corn dance, I saw in 1959 at Santo Domingo with its more than two hundred dancers, which taught me that Pueblo culture was not giving in to the onslaught of the twenty-first century; the solemn midnight Mass at San Felipe Pueblo on Christmas Eve, when buffalo and antelope dancers burst through the front door of the packed but quiet church, drums pounding, just as the Catholic priest stepped into the sacristy after communion; huddling at midnight in the frozen dark of the snowbound Hopi villages of Walpi and Hotevilla, lost and waiting anxiously for the bells and rattles of kachina spirits to guide us with ritual sonar through the ancient streets; and the silent moments alone contemplating the circular form of abandoned kivas or the massive adobe forms of Penitente *moradas*, long vacant but still somehow filled with the presence of earnest prayer.

Such experiences are part of the intangible reality of Albuquerque and New Mexico, and of other cities at the end of the world that have escaped to some extent the full influence of the evolving world culture of the late twentieth century.

Spiritual and other intangible realities are critical to a city's sense of place. Yet they are vulnerable, too, to trivialization and commercial exploitation. While it's impossible to "plan" for such intangibles, or to formally incorporate them into "urban designs," enlightened planners and policy makers will be sensitive to them. They will protect their material expressions and do nothing to hinder them. Making political and urban-planning space in which cultures and religions can flourish is to further a city's potential as a unique and valuable urban identity.

7

A City of Babel

AMONG the significant urban challenges of the 1990s in the Western United States is how to create a new public life from the burgeoning ethnic and socioeconomic diversity of contemporary cities. Sprawling cities that are built around the automobile tend to become compartmentalized in a way that compact, Eastern cities do not. Great distances and the isolation-booth quality of automobiles keep people apart. Community spirit is hard to maintain, especially if cities are growing rapidly and demographics are changing. Civic memory is lost. Established residents and immigrants alike tend to feel they don't belong to the city as a whole.

As a 1990 *Harper's Magazine* forum on creating public spaces declared, "public life is disappearing" in America. "It is strange that a nation so sentimental about its town meetings should be exposed—by apathy at home and the clamor of democratic throngs in the plazas of Europe—as having almost no public life."[1] One reason for this loss of community is the diversity of urban populations. Diversity not only results in cosmopolitan richness, it can also breed factionalism. And in some cities, such as Albuquerque, it has spawned a politics of apathy and babel. When Albuquerque created its "civic plaza" downtown in the 1970s, city leaders had hoped it would become a well-used public square, a meeting place for the entire city. It never turned out that way. Aside from its harsh and uninviting modernist design, the plaza couldn't act as a catalyst for public life because the concept of public dialogue and service was losing its power in America. The plaza became, instead, the site of pleasant, but largely commercial, cultural celebrations sponsored by the city on summer Saturday nights.

Albuquerque has been a city of babel since at least the end of World War II, and perhaps even before the coming of the railroad. It is a mobile American immigrant city.[2] Its population has grown by accretion, continually adding new people to its Indo-Hispanic and Anglo-settler base. Its fractured urban make-up is useful for understanding some of the general problems of communication in fast-growing, culturally fragmented urban environments.

In trying to create a new sense of community since the war, city leadership has taken a public-planning approach, nominally stressing citizen participation in the planning process. It has attempted to consolidate city and county governments. It created a city/county comprehensive plan, and focused considerable public money and attention on recycling its floundering downtown core into a center for the entire city. But the planning approach has not been successful. Two older, largely Hispanic parts of the metropolitan area have tried to become independent cities, disenchanted with city and county politics, charging tokenism in participatory planning. And consolidation has never been approved by county voters. Despite the best efforts of city leadership to conserve diversity and promote community, Albuquerque has not experienced a "confluencia"[3] of life-styles and cultures in its public life. To understand why these efforts have failed in this regard, it is necessary to explore the context that turns diversity into fragmentation.

For urban immigrants in the last twenty years, Albuquerque has often been a lonely place, filled with strange tensions, intimations of hostility, and the uncomfortable feeling that there's an unwritten code of conduct that no one will help you find or decipher. Still, it's a laid-back town, comfortably Western, and those taken for insiders appear to be happy and at ease, though oddly distant even if welcoming and friendly. Everyone seems to be speaking a different language, or not really speaking at all. And the physical city itself resembles a Chinese box of ingrown neighborhoods and districts all separated by superhighways, commercial strips, and formidable distances.

The first thing new businesses and families notice when they come to Albuquerque is that they're not alone. Newness in this old city is the way of life. The next thing they notice is that they're confused about where they really are.

Forbes magazine put it somewhat comically, saying "Albuquerque is torn between wanting to be part of the business mainstream and having a separate Wild West culture all its own."[4] A 1987 article in the magazine analyzed the results of a survey conducted to see which cities in the United States were the best and worst places for a marriage. Albuquerque was the worst. In reporting the findings, the Associated Press said that

> those surveyed found Albuquerque to be hostile to outsiders and complained that it had a bad effect on their children. . . . The place gives you a sense of being isolated, and it's more antagonistic, in a quiet way, than other large cities to people transplanted there from one

of the northern states or the East. Making friends of
your neighbors is no easy task.[5]

And yet a Rand McNally study in 1987 showed Albuquerque
to be one of America's "most livable cities."[6] Such contradictions are consistent with Albuquerque's historical crisis of
reputation and identity.

If Albuquerque is hard on newcomers and gives the im-
pression of hostile isolation, it's because factionalism in the
city is much more than a matter of ethnicity and socioeco-
nomics. It's endemic to both residents' public action and their
private lives. Albuquerque is a fractured city undercut by a
complicated variety of obvious and invisible divisions that
can be understood, in part, by one's becoming aware of the
creative tensions that shape the city's built environment.

The loneliness that newly arrived immigrants feel and the
seeming chaos of Albuquerque's urban form are strongly related. It's almost impossible, for instance, to achieve a working consensus on land-use issues in a city with little or no
public life. People tend their own gardens. It is of course
true, though, that the city has benefited from the sensitivity
and values of a few farseeing leaders in each generation. It
has had a steady professional planning bureaucracy since the
1950s. And it's been blessed with citizen volunteers who've
provided the momentum for everything from fine museums
and libraries to orchestras, open space, and the city zoo. But
modern Albuquerque has no enduring political matrix within
which public issues can be openly debated. The absence of
political dialogue is due in part to postwar nonpartisan politics at City Hall, which blurred social and land-use issues
in an effort to achieve consensus on economic-development
strategies. But Albuquerque's political numbness is mostly a

matter of urban character. Even with only slightly more than 500,000 people, Albuquerque is a city of islands—islands of culture, geography, language, politics, occupation, and economic class. People hole up here; they don't communicate. There is no common denominator, no sense of civic identity that all can share. The metro area is so balkanized, and so full of military and other transients and newcomers, that decision makers work virtually without public supervision, until they infringe upon the interests of one faction or another.

Albuquerque's leadership core is not large. And because Albuquerque is a political oddity, a burgeoning city without a visible power structure—without old money, powerful old families, political dynasties, and the like—the leadership core tends to be nearly as transient as the rest of the population. In recent years, power has floated, so to speak, among many elite groups and aggressive individuals. Leaders emerge—from the business world, public utilities, the university, the military/R & D community, and the legal profession—exercise control for a while, and then disappear again into their private lives and pursuits. Since World War II, engineers from Sandia Laboratories have played a consistent leadership role. And recently, former public-school officials have had considerable influence at City Hall. But the most historically persistent and organized faction in Albuquerque is that of land speculators, developers, the construction industry, banks, and savings and loans. A former city planning commissioner maintains that there has been no enduring political leadership in Albuquerque for the last twenty years but that "there was, however, a continuing, persistent development community. Politicians certainly have made compromises and decisions based both on their own philosophy and, unfortunately, at times for their own benefit economically or politically."[7] The city's 150 or so neighborhood associations try separately from time to time to provide a balance to development interests, but their efforts often end in futile and costly disputes over local zoning issues that frequently go to court. Neighborhood groups have seldom organized to promote political candidates or lobby for citywide planning initiatives.

Fragmentation in Albuquerque can best be understood if the city's factions are grouped into three general categories—contextual, cultural, and intellectual. The greater metropolitan area of Albuquerque has escaped the jurisdictional fracturing of many cities. Incorporated suburbs are not the plague they are elsewhere, owing to the deep poverty of most surrounding communities and their relative contentment with city and county services.[8] Nevertheless, it is not inaccurate to say that the city is more a loose confederation of contexts than a unified entity. Albuquerque does, however, have one all-pervading bifurcation common to most cities in the 1980s—the distinction between the poor and the well-to-do. The rate of poverty in the greater metropolitan area is the second highest in the Southwest, behind El Paso.[9] The reality of a chronic economic underclass makes the sociological tensions all the more volatile.

Greater Albuquerque is broken up into countless informal geographic and life-style contexts, and a number of institutional contexts as well. Like big-city neighborhoods, Albuquerque's contexts are more than just physical localities and islands of ethnicity; they are at once zones of interest and emotional homelands commanding powerful psychic allegiance. They are safe havens, hideaways in which to escape the isolation and emptiness of the desert and to protect oneself from the alienating speed of change that accompanies the boom-town growth of the city.

The contextual fragmentation is so intense in Albuquerque

that no unifying citywide planning is possible except under the guise of traffic engineering. And to make matters even more disjointed, people of specific contexts usually don't communicate with each other. Contextual factions wall themselves up in their sanctuaries and compete with each other for status and livelihood in the marketplace of this crossroads city. The Albuquerque area's nine city-council districts and five county-commission districts don't begin to represent all the city's contexts.

The city's geographic and life-style contexts include competing commercial zones such as Uptown, with its major shopping centers, office parks, and chain hotels; Downtown, with its dwindling retail base, its cultural institutions, and its huge eight-to-five population of governmental workers, secretaries, bankers, lawyers, and other professionals; Nob Hill, on mid Central Avenue east of the university, a reviving prewar neighborhood and part of the urban Main Street Program of the National Trust for Historic Preservation; North Fourth Street, a section of the sixteenth-century Camino Real to Mexico and now a country-funky commercial strip, with junkshops, feed stores, and fast food emporiums; the South Broadway area, with its renovated historic properties and disenfranchised Afro-American community; and the Academy area near the Sandias in the Far Heights, with its franchises and mountains of apartments and Cape Cod condos. And there are many more.

Life-style contexts include the independent-minded South Valley, largely in the county, largely Hispanic, largely working class, and mostly rural, the last near-town refuge, some say, of the free spirit of New Mexico; the North Valley, a semirural enclave of Anglos and Hispanics who vigorously defend their riverside life from the encroachment of developers and bridge builders; the University area, anchored by the school's nurturing campus environment and—with its book-stores, theaters, museums, and restaurants—the cultural hub of the city; Old Town, the original Albuquerque, founded in 1706 but annexed to the city proper only in 1949, now a tourist mecca of sorts, with fine museums and a grouping of neighborhoods that link the North and South valleys; the arid, volcanic Northwest Mesa and its residential archipelagos of middle-income New Mexicans and refugees from elsewhere, including Paradise Hills, Taylor Ranch, and Rio Rancho, which are among the city's most profitable "planned communities"; and the East Mesa with its San Fernando Valley ambience and congested California commercial strips.

Another group of contexts involves neighborhoods and communities, including outlying rural sanctuaries like the Village of Corrales, with its orchards, farmers, writers and artists, affluent doctors, good restaurants, and horse people. Corrales rests in the meadows and bosques of the Rio Grande flood plain north of Albuquerque, right below the sand cliffs and volcanic escarpment upon which sits the planned community of Rio Rancho. Here is a case study in isolation, emotional allegiance, and competing life-style contexts. Connected only by a two-lane country road, Rio Rancho and Corrales are literally worlds and centuries apart. Rio Rancho is a Rockwellian middle-class suburb, a former retirement community with club house and golf course that has turned into a principality of affordable housing. Driving down Meadowlark Lane from Rio Rancho into Corrales is like crossing a national frontier. One minute you're in Anyplace, U.S.A., the next you're cruising past adobe houses, Russian Olive hedges, and small corrals, right in the heart of romanticized New Mexico. One feels like Alice stepping through the looking glass, the transition is so dramatic and absolute.

In Albuquerque itself, so many life-style contexts exist that it's impossible to name or describe more than a fraction of them. Each neighborhood in the city, organized or not, seems to have its own character and fierce loyalty, as if it were the last bastion of sanity in a world shocked and frightened by the future. It's as true for my wife and me as it is for others. In our little corner of the mid North Valley, we live the privileged lives of urban rustics, cultivating our garden, surrounded by cottonwoods and a forest of elms, as inept at tilling as at adobe plastering, yet patriotically attached to our acre, crumbling house, cats, roadrunners, and the fragile ecology of life along the ditches. We've lived in this Eden for more than twenty years and the emotional bond between us and the land is so deep that subdivision developers with their seismic earth movers and war-zone noises can't begin to discourage us. We're not a neighborhood, but we are a context, an island of identity in a maelstrom of urban change. Larger neighborhood contexts include old Hispanic strongholds like Atrisco, Pajarito, and Barelas in the South Valley; Duranes, Santa Barbara Martíneztown, San José in the mid Valley; John Marshall, an Afro-American enclave on South Broadway near downtown; historic areas such as the Victorian Huning-Highland neighborhood, the turn-of-the-century Midwestern Downtown Neighborhood, the ambling, backroad–to–Santa Fe atmosphere of Guadalupe Trail, and the posh 1930s country-club district. Unfortunately, city officials tend to see Albuquerque's multitudinous neighborhood organizations as troublesome dissidents who get in the way of orderly growth and development. But with the absence of a formal growth-management plan for the city, self-protective neighborhoods are the only balancing influence capable of checking growth for growth's sake.

A second category of fragmentation in Albuquerque is a cultural one. While most major American cities are struggling to cope with cosmopolitan influxes from around the world and across the country, Albuquerque—at the end of the world though it may be—is paradoxically cosmopolitan by nature. Albuquerque has always been the site of conquests and migrations, from Anasazi settlers displacing Basketmakers in the tenth century, and the Spanish displacing Pueblo villagers in the sixteenth century, to Midwestern merchants angloizing Albuquerque in the late nineteenth century, and the military-industrial complex colonizing the town in the late 1940s.

The resulting cultural mix here is as exciting in its own way as that of a national capital. But our much touted triculturality—Indian, Hispanic, Anglo—is only a part of the picture. The term Indian, for instance, does not refer to a single culture but to three distinct ethnic groups—Navajo, Apache, and Pueblo. The Navajos, America's largest tribe, occupy parts of northwestern New Mexico, with isolated pockets in the central part of the state. Most Navajos live in Arizona. There are two basic kinds of New Mexican Apaches, the Mescalero and Jicarilla. Pueblo peoples are highly diverse. They speak three completely distinct languages—Zunian, Keresan, and Tanoan. And the three Tanoan sublanguages —Tiwa, Tewa, Towa—are mutually unintelligible as well. Along with Hopi speakers from Arizona, and the occasional Ute from the north, Native Americans play a vital part in Albuquerque's cosmopolitan nature. Hispanics, in their diversity, do as well. Native New Mexican Hispanics trace their ancestry to sixteenth-century Spanish explorers and settlers. They can be divided into two basic subgroups—those from Rio Arriba, up-river folks in northern New Mexico, and those from Rio Abajo, or down-river people. Some native Hispanics take pride in their pure Spanish descent, others in their mestizo background. Albuquerque also has a Mexican-American population, which came here first during the early nineteenth century and continues to emigrate from Chicano centers in Arizona and Southern California. There are also Mexican Hispanics, Puerto Ricans, Cubans, Central American refugees, and those from other South American nations.

Anglos in New Mexico have come to dominate the demographic landscape in the last thirty years with over 52 percent of the population. Hispanics come in at over 36 percent. Under the term Anglo, Spanish speakers used to group all non–Native Americans and non-Hispanics, including Afro-Americans and Asians. Anglos come from all states of the Union and many European countries. Some trace their descent from nineteenth-century mercantile, ranching, and farming pioneers, others from the thousands of health seekers who saw Albuquerque's climate as a cure for tuberculosis. But most came here after World War II. If Anglos have a subcultural identity in New Mexico that's distinct from national characteristics, it's based on either their romantic attachment to the New Mexican myth and state of mind, or on their colonial insensitivity to the local sense of place. Afro-Americans comprise less than two percent of the population, and are mostly clustered in Albuquerque and southern New Mexico. Many hail from local post–Civil War farming families, though a good number came to the state through the military. Albuquerque has had an influential Japanese-American community since World War II, many having been imprisoned in local internment camps. And since the Vietnam War, Albuquerque, like Los Angeles, has been the home of increasing numbers of Southeast Asians, as well as Hong Kong and Taiwan Chinese.

On a broader scale, Albuquerque's cultural fragmentation could also be defined in terms of general life-style. The city has a large number of Middle American apartment-dwelling and home-owning suburbanites, some die-hard urbanites always on the prowl for a big-city experience, and a diverse clutch of ruralites. These latter folk include small farmers and horse owners, rural villagers, and a large number of refugees from one kind of urban density or another, seeking the serenity and informality of New Mexico country living.

A final category of fragmentation in Albuquerque is intellectual, and this, as much as anything, accounts for the city's sense of loneliness and lack of community. Because of the state's geographic isolation, normal intellectual divisions are intensified, as much by the eccentricities of those who choose to live in the outback as by the introversion that results from working in a self-contained human oasis. The defense industry has brought Albuquerque and New Mexico more Ph.D.s per capita than any other major city in the nation. The University of New Mexico is itself an island of intellect in an ocean of real estate and commerce. The state is a mecca for painters, writers, musicians, and people with a hunger for history. Artists, physicists, humanities scholars, nuclear engineers, architects, composers, medical researchers, and physicians, (not to mention federal bureaucrats, lawyers, and members of the large financial, retail, and land development communities) all tend to cordon themselves off in intellectual ghettoes that keep them not only away from each other, but also too distracted to participate in the public life of the city.

One of the more lasting tensions that divides the city is between those who view Albuquerque as a marketplace and those who consider it a sanctuary. This conflict of perception is central to Albuquerque's political atmosphere as well as to its contradictory attitudes about growth. The city's population can be roughly divided into two types of people—those who see Albuquerque as a haven, an unfettered environment that stimulates innovation and originality, a reclusive paradise in which to live and work in freedom, a place to hide out from the pressures and conformities of American society;

and those who came here, or stayed here, to make it on their own, to succeed—who see the city as an arena of opportunity, an unencumbered frontier environment, a place ripe for progress to be shaped by entrepreneurial vigor. Both types have their negative side. The sanctuary mentality can lead to isolationism and rigidity. That's part of the reason why it's hard to get things done in Albuquerque. The spirit of the marketplace in this pioneer environment often engenders, on the other hand, a rapacious insensitivity to landscape and local culture, thus endangering the habitat that offers sanctuary. It should be noted that many people in Albuquerque could be placed in both categories simultaneously, exhibiting at once a progressive spirit and a respect and love for the New Mexican sense of place. It is also true that many people here belong to neither category, being military, corporate, or professional transients, or the homeless and working poor, who see Albuquerque as just another stop along the way.

This tension between sanctuary and marketplace has largely thwarted the city's attempt to create a new sense of community through participatory planning strategies. Long-range public planning has been highly successful in Albuquerque when it comes to open space, cultural facilities, parks, and historic preservation. It has proven less than adequate, however, in transportation planning, low-income housing, flood control, diversified economic development, and the prevention of urban sprawl. And it has contributed virtually nothing to creating a sense of unity and public spirit, in fact it's led indirectly to deeper divisions and greater fragmentation. A case in point is consolidation.

City leaders have submitted the proposed consolidation of city and county governments to county voters three times since 1953. The idea has been defeated each time. Ten years after the most recent vote in 1973, city leaders called for another consolidation study, but nothing came of it. And in 1990, the City Council passed a bill to study consolidation again. While some analysts claim that county residents worry about higher taxes and indifferent police and fire protection, I believe they reject consolidation because of life-style and land-use issues. Rural residents see planning as a threat to their traditional sense of place. They see growth and absorption into the city as destructive of the sanctuary quality of the North and South valleys and mountain communities. A consolidated city/county government also would probably mean a single metropolitan planning authority. And even though the city planning department already does all the planning for the county through a joint-powers agreement, a single authority seems ominously bureaucratic to many.

Consolidation's persistent defeat is also a symptom of Albuquerque's politics of babel. City leaders historically seem unable to comprehend the supreme importance that rural dwellers give to maintaining their life-style. Rural life in Bernalillo County has become a culture of its own, and one that cuts across ethnic lines and commands the most heartfelt allegiance. In the 1990s, backers of consolidation will have to prove to rural residents that bitterly contested actions such as the Southwest Area Plan and the Montaño Road Bridge, as well as a long history of flooding in the valleys, won't become the normal situation with a single metro government. These issues are symbolic of both the city's politics of babel and the conflict between the perspectives of those who value Albuquerque as a sanctuary and those who value it as a marketplace.

The Southwest Area Plan, known as SWAP, is part of the city's and county's comprehensive planning process. It took nearly three years to complete in the late 1980s and plans for the development of the South Valley through the year

2010, when the area's population is projected to have doubled to some 115,000 residents.[10] SWAP covers some 115 square miles, 95 percent of them in Bernalillo County. The area is largely rural and agricultural. Seventy percent of its residents are Hispanic. Despite intensive efforts on the part of planners, city staffers, and South Valley residents, SWAP turned into controversy rather than consensus. When the plan was completed, a coalition of residents took the drastic step of moving to incorporate the South Valley into a city they would call Las Plazas del Valle. As of this writing the incorporation is still in process. If residents are successful, Las Plazas del Valle would become the fourth largest city in the state.

South Valley residents thought the SWAP transportation plan endangered their rural life-style by imposing a grid system on the area's winding country roads and failed to provide enough bridges across the Rio Grande. In their minds, the road plan didn't conform to the South Valley's geographic or cultural terrain. They objected to its "assembly-line standardization."[11] Many residents also felt that the plan promoted the growth of the West Mesa at the expense of economic development in the valley. And they complained that the proposed road system would convey consumers over the valley to shopping centers in the Northeast Heights. One resident, Alex Saavedra, summarized the sentiment for incorporation, saying that "uncountable amounts" of money have been diverted from residents over the years

> to be spent on encouraging the development of Albuquerque's booming east side. Now, the shift of development to the west is threatening more years of lost revenue. Today, many segments of the South Valley continue to depend on backyard wells for water and septic

tanks for sewage, without benefit of tax money being channeled back into a proper sewage system.[12]

While residents in the South Valley revolted against what they saw as years of misunderstanding and neglect, North Valley homeowners challenged the city regarding plans for the construction of a bridge through their neighborhood and problems with chronic flooding. The similarity of issues in the North and South valleys is striking. The proposed Montaño Road Bridge—a two-lane, $20 million project connecting a portion of the West Mesa with major shopping outlets in the Northeast Heights—has been contested since at least 1969 by a coalition of small farmers, rural residents, low-income home owners, and relatively wealthy professionals who inhabit the Los Poblanos Historic District and the incorporated Village of Los Ranchos. Supporters of the bridge argued that rapid growth on the West Mesa made more bridges across the Rio Grande necessary, if the town wasn't eventually to be split in half by the river. Hardly anyone disagreed with the basic premise, but North Valley residents were convinced that bridges in their area would be used to stimulate growth rather than accommodate it. They argued that the bucolic quality of the North Valley was sacrificed for the economic development of the West Mesa. They also contended that the Montaño Road Bridge would destroy a vulnerable part of the Rio Grande bosque and damage important historic and archaeological sites. West Mesa motorists caught in rush-hour gridlock across existing bridges charged that North Valley residents were fat cats protecting their privileged turf. The battle over the bridge seems strange to South Valley residents who want more bridges, not fewer. But in the North Valley, fighting the Montaño river crossing became a matter of principle and even honor. Opponents felt that the integrity of their neighborhood was being threatened by insensitive bureaucratic forces that did not value its unique sense of place. Like South Valley residents, they chafed at what they considered disrespectful treatment and tokenism in the planning process—a process they participated in though, they charged, they were never listened to. Numerous suits were still in state and federal courts in 1990.

North Valley residents, even those who live within the city limits, generally oppose consolidation as well. They argue that the city and county can't provide them with basic services as it is, citing a long history of frequent and disastrous flooding during the summer wet season in poorer neighborhoods. After a torrential rain and widespread flooding in 1990, North Valley City Councilor Vincent Griego charged that the largely Hispanic valley had "been forgotten. . . . My question is, How much longer are we going to have to live with this?"[13] In a city that likes to keep up the appearance of ethnic harmony, Griego's remarks give a unique view of political frustrations in a city of babel. He was the only councilor to oppose a bill in 1990 that created another consolidation study committee.

A major emphasis on infill development in the City/County Comprehensive Plan—updated in 1987—focuses on the general ineffectiveness of planning when it comes to stimulating public spirit and a sense of community. In an effort to curtail costly urban sprawl, the plan advocates development on empty lots and parcels of land within the existing urban area. For most developers, however, savings on water and sewer extension fees are not sufficient to offset costly land prices. In order to turn a significant profit, residential infill developers regularly petition for variances in the zoning code to raise the number of allowable dwellings. In fact, infill development has come to mean an almost automatic rise in density. The Comprehensive Plan's emphasis on infill is largely rhetorical. It mandates no incentives for developers. This situation has created a continual zoning war between existing residents, who form neighborhood associations, and developers. In the fifteen years between 1975, when the plan was adopted, and 1990, nearly 150 neighborhood associations have further fragmented this already fractured city— and for a perfectly understandable reason. Property owners generally do not want higher-density new developments in their neighborhoods. Higher densities, they argue, change the basic character of their turf, congesting it with too many people, too many cars, and obtrusive, oversized buildings. While they don't object to infill in principle, they want it carried out within the standard requirements of the existing zone. It is the most basic and persistent conflict in the tension between sanctuary and marketplace. Planners, politicians, and developers tend to view zoning as an instrument of growth, amendable without much effort when improvement in the general economy is foreseen. Property owners see zoning as a defense against unwanted growth, as a protection of their neighborhood sanctuaries. To them, zone provisions should be amended only as a last resort, and only with the willing consent of existing neighbors.

This fundamental conflict is not unique to Albuquerque. It has caused innumerable disputes and lawsuits in other growing Western cities. But it is intensified in Albuquerque, I think, because of the city's long history of ethnic and linguistic diversity, as well as the tendency of many residents to keep closely to themselves and to identify with New Mexico's isolation and with the qualities of culture and landscape in their immediate environments.

Creating a public life from the political debris of rapid

growth in a city like Albuquerque seems next to impossible as we approach the turn of the century. But conditions similar to those in the 1970s—the heyday of political activism in Albuquerque—have been rising to national prominence again. When the Comprehensive Plan was adopted in 1975, America was in the middle of an environmental awakening. The plan itself was the product of more than six years of citizen involvement in a public-planning process which had given the city a sense of community that it perhaps had never had before. The plan's enlightened land-use, preservation, social, and environmental policies arose from the richness of the city's diverse points of view.

Creating a new public life from the environmental, social, and economic conditions of the 1990s is essential if cities are to be effective in attracting new business, combating pollution, paying the price for maintenance and repair of infrastructure, retrofitting themselves to make way for new transportation technology, and easing the social penalties of gross inequity that burden the working poor and homeless. If growing cities are not to become increasingly hostile and chaotic places, cities of Babel in which nothing can get done, public dialogue must be fostered, and welcomed, by elected leaders. And consensus must be gained.

Three lessons in the creation of community can be learned from Albuquerque's experience since the 1970s. First, a planning approach to creating public life does not work in lieu of a sincere welcoming of public debate by elected leaders. Comprehensive planning is based on dividing a city into major areas and sectors, thereby further entrenching fragmentation. Citizen participation in sector plans is orchestrated by technical staff who are not necessarily gifted at political interaction. In Albuquerque, productive citizen participation in planning seemed to end with the creation of the Comprehensive Plan itself. The political and public will did not exist to engage in the citywide dialogue necessary to continually update the plan. In a 1989 city-charter election, voters approved an amendment which requires an annual public-planning process to set five-year goals and one-year objectives. That seems to be a hopeful sign.

Second, to create dialogue in cities of babel, conflicting points of view must be institutionalized into urban political parties. And city councils and county commissions must be districted in such a way that related neighborhoods have elected representation. In Albuquerque, nonpartisan government is the rule. Political parties do not officially exist as far as urban issues are concerned. As a consequence, there can be no ongoing organized public debate about pressing concerns. Political memory on the part of the public is almost nonexistent. Memory is held by a restricted circle of political and bureaucratic insiders. And, intentionally or not, the public is excluded. Also, in Albuquerque, county commission and city council districts are so large that no elected official can adequately represent all the factions each one contains. The factions often become neighborhood associations to increase their visibility and power with elected and bureaucratic decision makers outside their general district, who set policy for the city as a whole.

Finally, a sense of community and public life can be fostered if citizen participation in the planning process is carried out in good faith and is not merely a token gesture to defuse immediate resentments and anxieties. Tokenism inevitably backfires. North Valley residents, for instance, did not begin as hard-and-fast opponents of the Montaño Road Bridge. They were invited to take part in transportation-planning discussions, but their position hardened into hostility when they saw that their involvement was treated as a political expedience, and that agendas were set and decisions essentially already made without them.

8

A City At the End of the World

WHEN seventeenth-century Spanish conquistadors described New Mexico as "a miserable kingdom" full of "backwardness" and "misery,"[1] they made what's probably a universal human association between distance and deprivation. The farther a place is from home, the farther it is from decency, civility, and the comely grace of "normal life." Being the back of the beyond, and "remote beyond compare,"[2] New Mexico has always suffered from this association. Americans today still disregard it as a parched, impossibly foreign place somewhere out at the end of the world. Of course, for those few who have found the normal life of their times to be barbaric, burdensome, or terminally boring, New Mexico's remoteness has been a treasured secret. And now, at the turn of the century in a world poisoned by waste and tormented by overpopulation, being "remote beyond compare" might prove to be a blessing beyond compare.

In such a context, Albuquerque's remoteness and obscurity is of excellent pedigree. By my reckoning, it is the most geographically isolated of any major city in the continental United States. It sits nearly in the middle of a state with the fifth largest land mass and with the eighth lowest density

135

of population—at 12.4 people per square mile.[3] The closest big city is Amarillo, Texas, nearly three hundred miles away. Denver, Tucson, Phoenix, Salt Lake City, Dallas, and Oklahoma City are all some five hundred to seven hundred miles distant. Albuquerque is also the commercial and population center of the most culturally exotic region in the country. Only Louisiana, I think, can rival New Mexico in political and social eccentricity. These qualities alone establish Albuquerque as a city at the end of the world.

Albuquerque's paradoxical nature also reinforces that status. The triple meaning of the image of "the end of the world" is particularly pertinent to the city's contemporary character. The image stands for seclusion, for an oblivion of distance and alluring enigmas, which provides the stimulus for utopian fantasies that allude as much to lost horizons as they do to promised lands. The image also connotes a sense of apocalypse, of the end of a millennium—a time of drastic and even catastrophic change. And there is in the image, as well, an ominous undertone of finality.

The unique circumstance of being a modern American city in the middle of a natural wilderness, and a precinct of historic and cultural authenticity, gives Albuquerque the best of all worlds, even though it is a far cry from self-important power centers, with their high-culture pretensions. Albuquerqueans live in both the city and the outback, in both the past and the present. It is, however, the city's relationship to the future that gives the triple meaning of the end of the world special poignancy and relevance.

For almost fifty years, since the explosion of the first atomic bomb at Trinity Site in southern New Mexico, the world has been poised on the brink of either finality or radical change. And Albuquerque has been a quiet but significant presence in the creation of this situation. More than any place in the Western Hemisphere, other than Washington, Albuquerque is the site in which the reasons for many of the worst fears of the postwar generations were created. Nuclear Doomsday, Armageddon, the balance of terror, the literal end of the world as we know it, was engineered and orchestrated in Albuquerque and in the mountains and deserts nearby. Even in the early 1990s, with the cold war over, not eighty miles away at the Los Alamos Scientific Laboratories, plutonium processing, taken over from the contaminated and discredited Rocky Flats plant in Colorado, was added to the Albuquerque areas's association with nuclear fears and mythologies. And Albuquerque remains the national headquarters for monitoring all defense-related nuclear materials in transit across the country, including those destined for the controversial Waste Isolation Pilot Project, or WIPP, outside Carlsbad, New Mexico. The state has made a good living off its Doomsday laboratories. At Albuquerque's Sandia National Laboratory, a new kind of living—from solar and nuclear fusion energy—is being tentatively explored. What a windfall it would be for Albuquerque to become, rather than the site of Armageddon research, the place where the world's hope of safe energy was made a reality.

When it comes to such images of the millennium, Albuquerque rises above its Strangelovian predicament. Albuquerque is a city uniquely positioned to capitalize on the revolutionary conditions of the immediate future, which will entail, I think, the end of the world's environmental and resource profligacy.

Up to the end of the 1960s, in the hottest part of the cold war, Albuquerque was one of countless American cities that paid little or no attention to its natural or cultural environments. It was the home of great scientific sophistication and pitiful urban blockheadedness. In 1965, urban critic Ian Nairn blasted the Duke City in his book *The American Landscape*:

> Albuquerque, for my money, is one of the stupidest wastes of human endeavor on this earth. It occupies a magnificent site between the Rio Grande and the Rockies. It pays no attention whatsoever to either, but simply goes on sprawling and spewing across the countryside in an endless repetitive pattern: without relationship, without identity.[4]

The comprehensive planning and open-space efforts of the 1970s and 1980s did much to stave off the full disaster that unchecked sprawl and designing against nature could have wrought on Albuquerque's long-term quality of life. At the turn of the century, after backsliding into the fantasy of affluence and unlimited plenty, like so many other American places in the 1980s, Albuquerque is poised, I think, to become a model post-end-of-the-world city—one that makes the most of being "remote beyond compare" by shifting the emphasis of its environmental public policies from consumption to conservation—the conservation and actualization of local identity.

For me, it's useful to look at cities metaphorically, to personify them and examine their development as one would consider the evolution and maturation of a personality. To achieve their full potential, cities, like people, must actualize their individuality, must discover and make the most of what they deeply and inherently are. With cities, the blossoming of local identity is synonymous with the blossoming of individuality or, as existentialist psychologists might call it, authenticity. For both people and places, authenticity requires introspection, candor, and a fundamental self-respect.

In Albuquerque, as in other fast-changing cities, the conservation and maturation of local identity depends, I think, on citizens and leaders embracing the concept of respectful growth. As I see it, respectful growth combines the economic and environmental perspective described by the term "sustainable development" with the human need to protect the emotional and cultural benefits of what's come to be known as "sense of place."

According to the 1987 World Commission on Environment and Development, sustainable development is growth "that meets the needs of the present without compromising the ability of future generations to meet their own needs."[5] In other words, to be responsible and farseeing, economic-development strategies in the 1990s and beyond must be grounded in the ethics of conservation—conservation of human and natural resources, conservation of landscape, and conservation of culture, which implies meeting the economic needs of all classes of people in a city.

While the kind of rapid growth experienced by Albuquerque, and much of the West since World War II, "means constant turmoil"[6] and must be avoided, economic growth itself is not an enemy of urban individuality, if it promotes what Santa Clara Pueblo architect Rina Swentzell might call loving change—development that is based on "continuing"—and shuns growth that promotes discontinuity.[7]

To nurture the blessings and mitigate the burdens of being a city at the end of the world is Albuquerque's great task at the turn of the century. And I believe opportunities will exist for it to succeed. The turn of the century will mirror, and perhaps intensify, conditions of the 1970s that were the catalyst

for many of the city's most farseeing and self-respecting conservation efforts. The economic hard times of the 1990s and
beyond will require a pragmatic, conservationist approach to
life—one that not only conserves natural resources, but that
conserves locality and its cultural and historic resources, as
well. In a general atmosphere of conservation, cultural and
aesthetic qualities can be seen as renewable resources too.

The timing is right for the citizens of Albuquerque-like
cities not only to choose a new future for themselves, but
to agree on a scenario for what that future will be. From
my point of view, that scenario arises from the evidence of
the present. The future will be characterized by increasingly
urgent environmental challenges and degradations; by dys-
functional big cities and the need to retrofit them to serve
growing populations and to operate on energy sources other
than petroleum; by an increasing resistance to monocultural
dominance, which will be accompanied by an assertion of
identity on all levels of locality, from nation to neighborhood;
by increasing interurban migrations of people and money; by
continued radical technological change; by increasing urban
violence; and by economic competition in a global urban
marketplace.

Another dominating feature of my scenario, as it relates
to Albuquerque, is the decline of Los Angeles. "People are
turning pessimistic about life in Los Angeles as the metropolitan area heaves against social strains of gang violence, rising
housing prices and traffic congestion made worse by growing
population," wrote Kevin Roderick of the *Los Angeles Times*.[8]
Journalist E. A. Torriero has used even stronger language,
saying that Los Angeles "is on the edge of catastrophe. . . . A
majority of Los Angeles County's 8.2 million people believe
their quality of life is declining at an alarming rate. . . ."[9] And
Ellen Uzelac writes, "The California dream is crumbling for

many, and studies show a caravan of Angelenos, fleeing to other states. . . ."[10] Although Albuquerque and the rest of the nation have much to learn from Los Angeles's efforts to control its growth and solve its water and air pollution problems, Albuquerque cannot afford to become a refuge for fleeing, laissez-faire Angelenos still harboring dreams of glory. The exodus of builders and developers could follow a trail to cities of least resistance, where they could continue the kind of hyped-up growth in urban size and density that eventually ruined Los Angeles.

To self-actualize in the context of this scenario, Albuquerque must get control of its national reputation and local self-image. This is not a cosmetic solution for deeper problems. How a city sees itself and how others see it has a profound influence on how it manages its growth, or if it does at all. Self-fulfilling prophecies affect cities as much as they do individual people. A city that wishes to maintain its local identity must be "visually 'imageable,'"[11] to itself and to others. It must observe itself and make the most of the distinctive images and symbols of its history as well as the defining landmarks of its geography, and use them to portray the expectations it has for its development. Such image making has little to do with creating a likeness of culture or making "quaintscapes," as in Santa Fe. Being able to manage growth means that leadership and citizens alike have an image of what they want their city to be. Without such an image, a city can't explain itself; it can't be known; it can only be treated as a nonentity, which means ultimately to be treated with disrespect.

To preserve its identity and husband its natural and civic resources, Albuquerque must find the courage to suspend peripheral development and control westward sprawl. Nothing threatens Albuquerque's sense of place, and its municipal integrity, more than California-style suburban development

on its western edges. Creating a huge new city far from existing civic services would put a tremendous burden on local
government. New cities which begin as developer-inspired
"planned communities" often fail to make it on their own
as revenue-generating municipal entities. And the big cities
they're associated with often have to rescue them at the taxpayers' expense.

If Albuquerque is to avoid becoming a "megapolis unbound," [12] it will have to restrain a cartel of land owners in the
geologically majestic, still virtually uninhabited, Rio Puerco
Valley. Development there could nearly double the size of the
city's physical dimensions and its population. [13] With questions being raised about Albuquerque's long-touted abundant
water supply, peripheral development takes on the air of fatal
absurdity. A 1989 study has shown that groundwater may
not be economically recoverable at lower depths, thus limit-
ing what once was thought to be an almost limitless supply
for development. [14] Although the Albuquerque Basin extends
from the Sandia Mountains to the Rio Puerco Valley, the Rio
Puerco does not share the Rio Grande's aquifer. Groundwater
in the Rio Puerco is not potable. There's even some question about the safety of Albuquerque's general water supply.
In 1990, a city/county committee studying the "vulnerability
of Bernalillo County ground-water resources" reported the
existence of more than 3,000 underground storage tanks in
the metro area, along with some 20,000 septic tanks, 17 land-
fills, and "about 300 facilities that reported they generate
some hazardous waste. Additionally petroleum product pipelines throughout the county transport about 19 billion gallons
annually." The committee found that "many commercial and
industrial facilities, including government facilities, throughout the County pose risks to ground water" from hazardous

wastes.[15] The vision of Albuquerque as an aquatic El Dorado is no longer supportable by even the most optimistic boomers.

By recognizing and responding to the troubles of the turn of the century, Albuquerque could become an inspiration for other localities which, as poet-farmer Wendell Berry says, have been "discomforted, disrupted, endangered, or destroyed by powerful people who live, or who are privileged to think that they live; beyond the effects of their bad work."[16] Localities need more than ever to take responsibility for the health of their natural resources and the usefulness of their urban form, and not give decision-making power to abstract market forces or high-image national corporations and governmental enterprises, whose names alone in the past have conferred legitimacy on the cities they inhabit.

Cities at the end of the world are one-of-a-kind places. Like all oddities, they are vulnerable to misunderstanding and disregard. If no one else cares much about them, at least their own people must—or risk the continual vanishing of the reasons they call such places home. In the 1960s, Albuquerque was, I think, as Ian Nairn observed, a stupid waste of human endeavor. It almost destroyed itself by sacrificing its authenticity in the hopes that conformity would breed prosperity. Instead, short-term growth came close to crippling the city's long-range potential. But important lessons were learned. The demolition of historic buildings, for instance, taught many people that once a building is gone it is gone forever. The same is true of a city. Once it sacrifices parts of its reality, it will never get them back.

Remote, endangered, at the end of the world, Albuquerque has survived the postwar boom, scarred and diminished, but with an authentic future still within its grasp. Surely, a place that so many love so fiercely, a place that is the chosen home of so many different kinds of people from such a variety of cultural and occupational perspectives, surely such a place will not betray its individuality. Our struggle must be to reconcile the forces of global change with those of local root-edness, character, and well-being.

Promises, Promises

IN THE EARLY 1990s, Albuquerque, New Mexico, seemed to me to be a unique city in the urban West. Unlike the senseless, sprawling uniformity that infected Phoenix, Tucson, Denver, Los Angeles, San Diego, and the fastest growing city in the nation, the waterless Las Vegas, Albuquerque was struggling inwardly to reach a consensus about respectful growth and maintaining its identity. It was still fighting the good fight to maintain itself as a modern New Mexican city, adapted to its natural and cultural contexts, and respecting the limits of both. It has never been an easy go for Albuquerque. Though the railroad arrived in 1880 and Route 66 went right through the heart of downtown in the early 1930s, Albuquerque was isolated by distance and culture from other major cities in the intermountain West and the West Coast. And its identity was confusing. A college town, a top-secret, high-tech, military enclave; a rural farming and ranching regional center; and the business capital of one of the poorest states in the nation, Albuquerque's eccentricities were tenacious and often crippling. And the chronic conflicts between urban and rural populations that make the legislatures of most western states something akin to madhouses, has been aggravated all the more by cultural differences in New Mexico. But New Mexico's and Albuquerque's poverty had always been counterbalanced, to some extent, by its position as the most foreign and arguably most culturally interesting of the fifty states, by the enormous intellectual firepower of national security laboratories and universities, by being the only indigenous Hispanic homeland left in the West, and the prime location of the only Native American tribes to have survived the onslaughts of European colonization while remaining more or less culturally intact.

Still Albuquerque's geographic isolation has always kept it out of step with national trends. As big cities in the West were disgorging out into their remaining countrysides from the 1970s through the 1990s, Albuquerque politics was at virtual deadlock between developers and conservationists. And now, at the turn of the century when many big cities in the West are realizing, belatedly and probably too late, that they have to manage their growth, Albuquerque is racing as fast as it can to the developable edges of town, despite threats of severe water shortages.

Its steady growth notwithstanding, Albuquerque never had an LA-style, Denver, Las Vegas, Phoenix kind of boom. Its real estate prices never inflated, and then imploded, like LA's after years of overbuilding and overpricing its housing stock of mansions. It never had the fortunes that Colorado's mining traditions left Denver so it could recreate its downtown, airport, and stadium as the symbols of success in the Rockies. It never had the southern-like refrigerated-air society of Phoenix, with its culture of newcomers, its retirement appeal, nor its proximity as a virtual bedroom community to San Diego and LA, and its laid-back, affluent, golfing atmosphere so appealing to those who man corporate headquarters. And it never had the glamour nor the economic clout of Las Vegas, which brought the entire state of Nevada into servitude to help keep that state's economic dynamo growing and growing faster than anyplace in the West. And it really never had Tucson's proximity to Mexico, its eco-activist association with Ed Abbey or Joseph Wood Krutch, or its close but competitive relationship with a major city like Phoenix and its seemingly unstoppable growth machine.

But even now in this time of sprawl, Albuquerque has one major asset that distinguishes it from these and other western cities—the unequaled vastness, variety, and endless magnificence of the New Mexican landscape, which still has, despite the Albuquerque–Santa Fe corridor, the wonderful and paradoxical feeling of a civilized wilderness, wild but deeply cultured.

For over thirty years as a journalist, I've tried to look at Albuquerque's built environment as a natural resource modified by human choice in this most spectacular and humblingly beautiful setting. In well over 1600 columns in many publications I've tended to portray Albuquerque as a lovable, even wonderful place, for all its foibles and follies. Ten years ago, when this book was first published, I saw Albuquerque as being one of those rare forgotten cities with most of its great potential still to be realized. Now, I'm not so sure—though some things certainly never change.

If you think the subtitle of this book, *A City at the End of the World,* seems a bit over the top, consider that the *New York Times* in October 29, 2001, ran a map in which the state of New Mexico was mislabeled as Arizona.[1] Arizona itself was left unlabeled, and New Mexico was relegated so far to the end of the world, it tipped over into the realm of nonexistent places. And Albuquerque, of course, is the biggest city in that missing region we call the Land of Enchantment. Some on the East Coast might think such a term of endearment was chosen to represent a fantasy, a Never-Never Land, too enchanting to exist. Tragically, many in Albuquerque still seem to think so too.

In the decade since the book was published, the people who think of New Mexico as an empty space waiting to be filled with generic corporate gimcracks and the marketing fruits of bad ideas that have cluttered up the rest of the nation and the West with a babble of strip malls, neon commercial graffiti, and sprawling suburbs appear to be winning the war for Albuquerque's identity. And I have to admit I'm really not sure why.

Ten years ago I thought that Albuquerque was "poised . . . to become a model post-end-of-the-world city—one that makes the most of being 'remote beyond compare' by shifting the emphasis of its environmental public policies from consumption to conservation—the conservation and actualization of local identity."[2] I think I was wrong. Instead of actualizing its individuality, and making the most of its cultural complexity, arid limitation, and vast natural beauty, Albuquerque's built environment has slipped ever more closely into becoming indistinguishable from the anonymous edges of any one of a hundred other western American car towns. But I have to say, too, I don't think that was the city's deep intent. Albuquerque's urban landscape has not only languished in a mire of unfulfilled promise, but that unsettling disappointment has also been punctuated by rare, but heartening, surprises.

Who would ever have guessed that hidden in the smoggy atmosphere of dispiriting stagnation, Downtown Albuquerque, after more than thirty years of desolation, would actually be revived, somewhat, with a major new movie house, an Alvarado Hotel-like transit center, and three new courthouses?

It's been a shock for many to realize that, at the beginning of the new millennium, the leading urban clients for modern New Mexico design strategies are the formerly impoverished Pueblos of Santa Ana, Sandia, and Isleta. (In our state, it seems, though, that everything good comes with its painful barbs and stickers, in this case gambling casinos and a glut of Pueblo resorts and golf courses.)

And it feels almost unnatural that in our deeply libertarian, boom-town atmosphere two progressive urban think tanks—Shared Vision, Inc. and 1000 Friends of New Mexico—would have arisen to try to bring some sanity to our development patterns, or that City Hall, County Government, and citizens could have created a 750-page "Planned Growth Strategy," emphasizing infill rather than sprawl development, which many elected officials and business people say they like.

Who would have thought that the Twin Mountain Construction

Company and the New Mexico State Highway Department could have redesigned and rebuilt, with minimum hassle and wasted time, something of a masterpiece of aerial roadways to replace the old eyesore of the Big I crossroads of I-40 and I-25? And who's not surprised that the hated Montaño Road Bridge, for forty years the object of raging political battles, would actually get constructed and become not only a monstrous gusher of unregulated gridlock into the rural North Valley, but would also, ironically, be one of the more beautiful bridges in the state?

I would never have bet that state land commissioner Ray Powell could have partnered with Sandia National Laboratories and the Department of Energy to design a 2800-acre nature refuge and environmental education campus on the eastern edge of its Mesa del Sol development next to Isleta Pueblo land. And I couldn't have really imagined ten years ago that the Nob Hill Main Street Project would create a massively successful and energetic shopping and eating zone, anchored by a local eatery called Flying Star, which competes successfully with anything in the northeast heights.

Perhaps the greatest and happiest surprise is a work of community-designed affordable housing and infill called Arbolera de Vida. Located in the Old Town area's Sawmill District, on the old Duke City Lumber Yards, the Sawmill community advisory council worked with the City of Albuquerque, which owned the twenty-seven-acre project site, to create a model infill development for low-income New Mexicans. The city and Sawmill residents developed the Sawmill Community Land Trust, a private nonprofit corporation to hold the land for the community. The Trust prohibits real estate speculation and absentee ownership, keeping houses affordable over many generations, and guaranteeing community control of design. The residents of the Sawmill neighborhood, and city planners, have given everyone in Albuquerque solid proof that it's possible for local interests to engage in respectful growth and to defeat the deadening forces of generic economics and design.

But even with these sweet amazements and startling successes, Albuquerque's promise as a unique city is starting to be overwhelmed by generic change that pays no attention to the ecological realities of our fragile landscape and chaotic weather patterns—just like Los Angeles and Phoenix two decades ago and Las Vegas, Nevada, today. We know that, despite the appearance of the 1000 Friends of New Mexico, "smart growth" is not a term warmly embraced by the power structure here. And that coolness comes even in the face of the "Beyond Sprawl" managed-growth initiative by the Bank of America in California and New Mexico in mid-1995. Even a major lender with a considerable and at times decisive role to play in our city's growth couldn't change minds here. We know that despite a genuinely progressive young mayor in Los Ranchos, John Hooker, who fills public debate with arguments about "new urbanism" and the creation of self-contained developments, designed to cut down on commuting and car travel, few with clout in Albuquerque, other than defeated-mayor Jim Baca, take that seriously either.

With the exception of Baca's four-year tenure in the late 1990s and his deft orchestration of the revival of downtown, none of the old agenda of the 1970s, outlined so clearly in the much updated and amended Albuquerque/Bernalillo County Comprehensive Plan, has yet to be fulfilled.

In fact, it seems that all through the 1990s, during one of the greatest booms in American economic history, Albuquerque decided neither to focus on shoring up its New Mexican authenticity, despite planning mandates to do so, nor to adapt its water usage to its desert climate. Albuquerque's elite didn't have to do anything innovative at all to get richer. Nor did the historical circumstances of the 1990s present the city's leadership with the kind of direct challenges that stimulate productive change, except, of course, for the looming crisis of water scarcity, which only in the new millennium began to be timidly and haltingly addressed.

No one I've talked to over the last thirty years of observing

Albuquerque politics has much of a clue about how land-use and other environmental decisions are really made here. And neither do I. We all know, of course, the functions of the various governmental agencies and committees, but the Wizard of Oz remains hidden. And except for population size and general sprawling expansion, nothing much seems to change, or really has changed since the 1950s. The pattern here is that when land development clashes with cultural passions and environmental imperatives it adapts itself to the obstructions, flows around them, and then prevails and keeps moving relentlessly on. Mayors and city councils come and go, business leaders hoist a corporate hero who makes pronouncements and then moves to another city, inspired planners and powerful deans of the UNM School of Architecture and Planning articulate grand visions and are forgotten, neighborhood advocates and managed-growth activists rise up and are heard and then subside exhausted. Frustrated bigwigs and dealmakers complain bitterly that Albuquerque's growth is stalemated by conflict, but that's an illusion. Just look at how the city's grown. No place is free from regionally unresponsive generic development. No part of the city is free of sprawl.

How then are land-use decisions made? Though I'm groping around in the fog like everyone else, it seems not unlikely to me that the answer is something like this: First, the leadership community works in mysterious ways because it is, itself, deeply fragmented and diffuse, reflecting Albuquerque's overall status as a City of Babel. Second, New Mexico's general impoverishment allows many decisions to be made almost by default without the kind of governmental oversight that's needed. And, third, Albuquerque's major news outlets—the *Albuquerque Journal* and electronic media that use it as a news source—are so unreflective and growth oriented that land-use issues hardly ever furrow their collective editorial brows.

Fragmentation and unaccountability are the easiest to analyze.

Albuquerque City Government is nonpartisan. No national political party is attached to any land-use decision. The buck stops with no one. Coalitions are hard to build. Policies are often developed ad hoc. The closest thing to an enduring land-use lobby comes from development interests who've been pushing the same uncontrolled growth agenda, and opposing virtually any and all regulation, for the better part of fifty years. The electorate is kept at bay by a regional planning body called the Middle Rio Grande Council of Governments (COG), which produces virtually all transportation studies and masterminds all transportation decisions through a committee known as the UTPPB or Urban Transportation Planning Policy Board, comprised of elected officials from virtually every jurisdiction in the region. These elected officials, however, have no region-wide constituency, each coming from a particular town, city, county, or tribe. Hence they are accountable to no general electorate for decisions that affect the whole Middle Rio Grande metro area but perhaps benefit only one area to the detriment of many others. It doesn't help, either, that UTPPB members serve all but anonymously, thanks to the aversion to local news evidenced by most major print and electronic media here. And the UTPPB has never seen a road it doesn't love. When you combine the workings of the UTPPB with county and city environmental planning commissions in Albuquerque, Rio Rancho, and four counties, all of which are composed mostly of people who make their living selling or developing land, then add to this mix a fragmentation of business organizations, which include multiple chambers of commerce, Rotary clubs, the Albuquerque Economic Forum, and other groups, and a vast but hopelessly fragmented body of some 130 neighborhood associations, not to mention such arcane political entities with enormous clout over water like the MRGCD (The Middle Rio Grande Conservancy District) and AMAFCA (the Albuquerque Metropolitan Arroyo and Flood Control Authority), you see what a mess it is.

Is it any wonder that normal citizens, whom polls have shown for years are opposed to sprawl and rapid growth and favor slower more considered infill development, feel they're never taken into account when land-use decisions are being made—unless of course they take developers and politicians to court? When voters are ignored, their only recourse is to change roles and become plaintiffs.

So it's no surprise, then, that in the last ten years, none of the old political land-use controversies were resolved, especially the consolidation of city and county governments, which the leadership elite has pushed for years and the newly elected mayor, centrist Democrat Martin Chavez, has pledged to make a reality, despite the bitter protest of county voters.

But while the city grows and public policy stumbles along, staggering new problems, long unattended to, are, indeed, now slowly breaking into public consciousness. These new problems are symbolized by water warfare among towns and cities, farmers, Native Americans, and environmental interest groups and massive new developments on the far edges of town. If ever evidence were needed that the years and years of environmental planning and general palaver about growth, and the ecological stress that comes from too much of it, have come to little or no avail, look far, far west, and far, far east.

The Albuquerque Academy's Mariposa development with its seven thousand proposed houses in an "environmentally sensitive planned community" on the outer limits of Rio Rancho near US 550, almost halfway to San Ysidro, touts itself as having learned the necessary lessons about smart growth and new urbanism. And perhaps it has. The only problem is that it amounts to the farthest vanguard of urban sprawl in the history of westside development. It's so far from other houses or any jobs that residents there could end up being stranded in their luxurious sensitivity during an oil crisis as severe as those of 1974 and 1979.

Or take the proposed Campbell Ranch development on north

Highway 14 in the East Mountains, with its hotels, golf courses, and thousands of houses on eighteen thousand acres. In what's been called "one of the most extraordinary moments in the history of local government,"[3] Campbell Ranch, after concluding that Bernalillo County planning regulations were too restrictive, petitioned successfully to be annexed into the town of Edgewood in the Estancia Valley many miles from its development site. There's never been an annexation like it. Talk about stretching a point! And Edgewood, as of January 2002, was being sued by Santa Fe County to make sure the town has the money it will take to provide all the services Campbell Ranch will need, so county government won't have to.

Former Mayor David Rusk, who lost his bid for reelection in 1981, once argued that Albuquerque's metro area growth was uncomplicated by the same kind of jurisdictional fracturing that plagues Denver, Los Angeles, and other western cities. When it comes to sheer volume of jurisdictions, that's still true. But both governments and citizen action groups in Rio Rancho, Placitas, Corrales, Cedar Crest, Tijeras, Los Lunas, Belen, Bosque Farms, Edgewood, Sandoval County, Valencia County, Torrence County, and Sandia, Laguna, Santa Ana, and Isleta Pueblos make enough of a jurisdictional jumble that it's hard even for nationally dominant corporations, at times, to get much done in our area. Even Wal-Mart failed in the late 1990s to get a foothold in the Village of Tijeras, largely due to the opposition put up by the extremely well-organized, conservation-oriented neighborhood group called the East Mountain Legal Defense Fund [EMLDF]. But Albuquerque and Bernalillo County's urban form, and all their official efforts to contain sprawl, were thwarted when Intel, the largest computer chip manufacturer in the world, bought land in, and was feasted with $8 billion in industrial revenue bonds by, Sandoval County right on the Bernalillo county line.

While, to the casual observer, Albuquerque and environs might still look pretty much the same as they did in 1992, if not slightly worse, beneath the physical and political surface vast forces of change are at work, and like it or not, one day every government in the area will have to respond to them.

I'm intrigued by the coincidence that the two most dramatic forces of change—the realization of water scarcity and the appearance of Pueblo governments as major players in urban development—began almost simultaneously, and oddly unnoticed, during the tenure of the all but invisible mayor of Albuquerque, Democrat Louis Saavedra, who served four years in the late 1980s and early 1990s, and the almost insane first term of another all but invisible politician, Republican Governor Gary Johnson, who ends eight years in office in 2002. As the story goes, Mayor Saavedra, wanting to avoid major political struggles over water conservation, decided to conduct a study instead, the first one of its kind, measuring Albuquerque's aquifer using USGS monitoring devices in city wells. As the data began to add up it became clear to hydrologists at the USGS that Albuquerque was not sitting atop a body of water the size of Lake Superior, as city boomers had always claimed. Rather it was draining a number of relatively small deep pools of water—one near Kirtland Air Force Base in the southeast heights and the other near the Ladera section of the West Mesa—much faster than previously thought. When that story was first reported in 1989 by Tony Davis of the *Albuquerque Tribune,* hardly anyone paid attention to it. It took almost the whole decade for city officials and Albuquerque's invisible leadership community to realize that our area is running out of water now. And many still don't believe it.

The other profound unintended consequence of political maneuvering was when the then young Governor Gary Johnson rammed through what turned out to be an unconstitutional set of compacts with some nine Rio Grande Pueblo governments to allow "indian gaming." Johnson could not have imagined in 1996 that Pueblos around Albuquerque would become so wealthy, and be so well managed financially, that their own development efforts could well become the single most determining factor in Albuquerque's urban form over the next fifty years.

I'm not suggesting, though, that nobody saw Albuquerque was facing major problems long ago. In 1986, the *Albuquerque Tribune* published a twenty-four-page pullout section called "Albuquerque 2000."[4] This set of analyses, more than any other, reveals that Albuquerque has done almost nothing to alter its growth and land-use policies to fit contemporary conditions. In 1986, the city was working off plans, concepts, and aspirations that were at least thirty years old. And I think it's safe to say that we're still operating on that same view of the world at the start of the new millennium. In 1986, The *Tribune* predicted Albuquerque's water supply would be drying up and full of contamination by the turn of the century. "Water might even have to be pumped from the San Juan Basin, near Mount Taylor, to satiate development on the West Mesa," The *Tribune* observed with prescience. It added that "until the pocketbook dictates water use practices, it will be tough to change Albuquerque attitudes. But conservationists believe the effort should begin now." Albuquerque still has some of the least expensive residential water in the Southwest. And what conservation has been practiced in the last fifteen years or so has been offset by population growth stimulated by sprawl development that's been speeded up by roads and bridges that were sold to voters as solving rush hour congestion, but really only jammed roadways all the more.

Maybe it's just me, but trying to find a clear stream of logic running through the last ten years of Albuquerque's urban history, I keep running into streams of cause and effect as clogged up as Coors Boulevard at rush hour. Perhaps one useful way to get at what's happened in the years since those *Tribune* predictions is to concentrate on three polarized situations: First, two competing plans with major potential influence, a transportation plan that seems like a holdover from the Eisenhower era, and a planned growth strategy that appears simultaneously to be the new embodiment of the antisprawl progressive spirit of the 1970s, but a too-little-too-late token gesture at managed growth; second, two looming scarcities, oil and water, and how they relate to the first two plans; and third, two approaches to development, the Pueblo approach and the developer-led, bottom-line, laissez-faire approach on the West Mesa with its mile after torturous mile of miserable nonsense roads.

As Alan Reed, former Albuquerque City Councilor and prominent member of the 1000 Friends of New Mexico, wrote in the organization's newsletter, *Nuestro Pueblo,* the New Mexico State Highway Department's "Middle Rio Grande Connections" study is full of "loops to nowhere."[5] And yet the "connections" study could become the underlying growth blueprint in the metro area for generations. A major recommendation of the study, which calls for building a superhighway called Paseo de Volcan west of Unser on the West Mesa, was approved by a 12–7 vote by the UTPPB in mid-January 2002. As there's not a living soul anywhere in sight out there, Paseo de Volcan, a so-called loop road connecting I-40 with US-550, is a pure and simple golden gift to developers from the taxpayers of New Mexico, a sprawl subsidy that really no one who follows the weather, the economy, the water crisis, or the news about extended long-term war in oil country in the Middle East would ever dream of suggesting.

And that's not all. There's another proposed road that's truly "shocking," according to Reed. The Middle Rio Grande Connections "seriously advocates building two freeways between I-40 west of Albuquerque and NM [*sic*] 550 . . ." The second loop road is so far west of the Double Eagle II airport it doesn't really have a name. Reed, a Democrat turned Republican, estimates the cost at about $12 million per mile, "leading to a $240 million bill for the short freeway (Paseo de Volcan) and about $500 million for the longer freeway. The traffic demand," he says, on the shorter road "would amount to less than two percent of all interstate traffic!

This leads us to the conclusion that there is little traffic justification for either of them. The only apparent beneficiaries would be land developers along the routes."

The spin argument that loop roads provide a development boundary for a city has long ago been debunked. Loops simply make it possible for development to occur both inside them and outside them to a virtually limitless degree, often extending the outer edge for miles. Reed is right, of course, about the complete lack of current traffic justification for those roads. North Unser Boulevard, the farthest road west at the moment, is a lovely, wide winding road through some eighteen miles of utterly barren and supremely beautiful New Mexico countryside. You can pick it up past Southern Boulevard and drive all the way to US 550 and pass by only one little island of houses, connected by one forlorn little road. The irony is, or course, that Unser along this stretch is about the best road on the whole, overstuffed westside nearer the river.

Despite virtually every other article in the daily papers dealing with impending water shortages, despite being worried about depleted oil reserves and an uneasy dependence on foreign oil, even Democrats are hot for westside roads. Mayor-again Marty Chavez, whose first term and second term are separated by the Baca administration, has vowed to do everything he can to extend Paseo del Norte through the Petroglyph National Monument and hook it up with a completed Unser. And that's despite continuing and strenuous objections from Pueblos who consider the site, and its "rock art," sacred ground for all the pueblos up and down the Rio Grande. Considering that the major pueblos in the Albuquerque area have unadjudicated senior water rights, and enough money to defend them forever in the courts, one wonders why the Albuquerque mayor would offend their religious traditions. New Mexico's Republican Congressional delegation has already attacked Sandia Pueblo's claim to the northwest side of the Sandia Mountains, using language that implied nefarious dealings, charges that I'm sure no pueblo person will ever forget.

Ironically, the most newsworthy opponent of the Paseo del Norte extension through the Petroglyph National Monument is a national environmental group called Republicans for Environmental Protection. Jim Scarantino, president of the New Mexico Chapter, sees the roadway as an instrument of sprawl just as 1000 Friends does. "One of the dirty little secrets about sprawl is that it's a taxpayer ripoff," he's quoted as saying.[6] Characteristically, the very conservative *Albuquerque Journal* was outraged, in an editorial entitled "When Enviros Protest Cost, Be Suspicious," that any environmental group, Republican or not, should attach a taxpayer price to a road extension.[7] In Albuquerque, loyalty to the sprawl lobby comes even before party loyalty, or so it seems.

If transportation planning has always been a spur to booming sprawl development, what's known loosely as "comprehensive planning" has been something of a restraining force. Since the 1970s, all versions of the Albuquerque/Bernalillo Comprehensive Plan have mandated that infill development be given at least equal priority to growth on the fringes where roads and water and sewer lines, and police and fire protection, are nonexistent and must ultimately be paid for by taxpayers. Infill means not only using up vacant land, but also maintaining the public resources and infrastructure that already exist within the city's developed core, much of which is decaying.

The Comprehensive Plan was always an inspiration to conservationists, but it had, as the saying goes, no teeth, no laws or incentive strategies to encourage infill. In 2001, another comprehensive planning document appeared, all 750 pages of it, that assigns priority to infill development. It's called The Planned Growth Strategy and is a joint effort by Bernalillo County and the City of Albuquerque.[8] This massive undertaking has what it calls seven basic ideas[9] gleaned from town hall meetings, citizen surveys, planning and engineering consultants, and existing planning documents. No one has any idea, of course, if this document and its suggestions will be any more fruitful in directing growth to serve public needs and ease taxpayer expenses than the efforts of the 1970s. But I'd rather play the slots at a casino than bet it will.

Under the heading "What the Public Told Us They Wanted," the seven basic ideas are: 1. "Local government should play a proactive role." This means that city and county officials should try to help developers stick to the strategies' view of growth. 2. "Whether in new or older area, not just development but *community.*" This seems to be inspired by a "new urbanist" emphasis on village-style development, emphasizing pedestrian environments. 3. "The existing community—neighborhoods, schools and businesses—comes first in vitality and development." I presume this is an infill development mandate. 4. "Maintain, rehabilitate, & improve infrastructure in existing neighborhoods." 5. "Grow efficiently—develop first where infrastructure exists." 6. "Don't just plan—implement." And 7. "Keep us involved—every step of the way."

In Part Two of the Planned Growth Strategy, the "Preferred Alternative," a call is made for "an urban development paradigm shift."[10] Albuquerque's "existing paradigm for urban development is that government will be responsive to incremental private development initiatives with limited controls to avoid negative consequences." Infrastructure planning is basically "reactive." "The City water and sewer utility currently has no procedure to estimate the cost-effectiveness of service expansions. . . . Urban development at the fringe largely is developer driven." This "reactive and piecemeal approach" has resulted in, among other things, over-crowded schools and streets "in growing fringe areas; . . . [and] a more than $700 million dollar backlog of infrastructure deficiency projects, deficiencies in the street system which exceed the cost of supporting new urban development for the next 25 years. . . ."

While developers seemed at first to be oddly unperturbed by these suggestions, they soon saw them as the thin edge of the wedge when it comes to managed growth, which always has been an anathema to them. Initially, they saw The Planned Growth Strategy as, indeed, a growth-oriented plan of attack. It was only later that they began to loudly object to giving infill priority status. In the beginning, "developers and 'smart growth' advocates agree," according to a report by *Albuquerque Tribune* business reporter Nancy Salem.[11] The Home Builder's Association of Central New Mexico thought the plan made sense because it supported predictable, stable growth and "growth generates income." The smart growth oriented 1000 Friends of New Mexico seems to like it for its balance. More progressive water conservationists, on the other hand, think it's all a bunch of baloney, because they see little or no discussion of water in the plan.

The developers and their lobbying organizations were at first unfazed by the Planned Growth Strategy's emphasis on building in areas with existing infrastructure because most of the low-cost fringe development in the future will take place outside of Albuquerque and Bernalillo county—in Sandoval, Santa Fe, and Torrence Counties, and in Rio Rancho, and Los Lunas and Belen— and, therefore, beyond the jurisdiction of the plan. But they vigorously attacked the plan, it seems, when it dawned on them that it set a precedent for sustainability in the Middle Rio Grande Valley. This was yet another anathema. If an infill priority is killed in Albuquerque, they must have reasoned, sprawl will probably have its way here until the sands of drought cover over the Big I.

For instance, some of the most beautiful and spiritually inspiring landforms on the planet, with views across the Santa Ana reservation to the Jemez Mountains on US 550, are about to be despoiled by Rio Rancho developers, once those new western loop roads are built. Any development out there amounts to a desecration, as far as I'm concerned. I always used to take out-of-town friends and family up US 550 to look at the view as you topped out onto what we think of as the Zia/Santa Ana Valley with its long view of the red cliffs of the Jemez and gray-and-white-banded badlands stretching northwest from San Ysidro. That "viewfield," as planners and builders call it, is irreplaceable and every bit as startling and monumental as the view of the Sandias from the opposite direction. It's been a nasty surprise to watch the land approaching that view get bulldozed over, transformed into a red dust, Martian no-man's-land. But perhaps, in the odd way the world works, what to some people is an unthinkable calamity will rescue those desert views from the depredations of suburbia.

The unthinkable might, indeed, be upon us. Both current transportation planning and managed growth strategies could well run up against the inevitable bottoming-out of the basic resources of oil and water. And in overbuilt, arid, vast central New Mexico a shortage of either one is a disaster, while a shortage of both could amount to what corporate merger masterminds might call the "creative destruction" of our present state of old-fashioned thinking.

Will the world find itself in a price-spiraling oil crisis anytime soon? It didn't take much in 1974 and 1979 for shortages and high prices in imported petroleum to reverberate destructively through the whole American economy. And in New Mexico, the effects were close to crippling, even then when the vast majority of our metropolitan population was still living within the core area. Unlike today, the far fringes of the desert and the mountains, miles away from jobs and essential retail centers, were still reserved for pioneers and easterners who didn't know any better. But I get nervous when I stumble across book reviews and articles that refuse to deny the possibility of a major oil shortage coming from war and social unrest in the Middle East. And I get really upset when I see book reviews of obscure but highly credible texts like Kenneth S. Deffeyes's work from Princeton University Press called *The Impending World Oil Shortage*. An oil geologist turned Princeton professor, Deffeyes, according to reviewer J. R. McNeill in the *Wilson Quarterly*,[12] predicts that "world oil production will peak between 2004 and 2008 and decline thereafter, with potentially calamitous consequences." I can just smell the carcasses of rotting SUVs all over Rio Rancho and the East Mountains. An oil crisis in Albuquerque right now would leave everyone hurting, and tens of thousands all but stranded in their commuter exurb utopia.

And I can't imagine what might happen if oil prices up the costs of trucked-in food so much that poor people here have a harder time making ends meet, especially if Albuquerque and Rio Rancho and big developments on the fringes are buying up water rights from farmers. With various PR machines still grinding out enticements for businesses and homeowners to move to our city, I wonder sometimes if we'd have enough wet water left to grow our own food if we needed to?

But despite my own dark broodings, when it comes to thinking about water, Albuquerque is in an entirely different state of mind than it was ten years ago. From my perspective as a columnist the water scene looks fairly straightforward, even if agencies, corporate bureaucracies, activists, and politicians all try to mess it up with funny money numbers. It's hard to pin anyone down on exact figures. But it doesn't take a statistician to see that the overall picture isn't very good for growth, or for just simply watering our lawns and trees.

Even though such a venerable thinker about land speculation and ranching as former Governor Bruce King once told me, "V. B., ya can always find more water," many conservationists and people in state government, and in city and county agencies all over New Mexico, are worried that there really might not be enough water to go around anymore. They fear that the humane idea of "shared scarcity" could get pulverized by the win/lose water combat ahead. They know the era of federal water projects is over. There are no new rivers to dam. Generally speaking, all the water in the West is already spoken for. So is there anyplace left to turn? For some prominent thinkers, agricultural water is the great hope of cities and developers. For farmers, though, cities seem like cartoon vultures licking their chops.

William Riebsame, a professor of geography at the University of Colorado, Boulder, figures that "if half the agricultural water use in the West shifted to urban uses, the region could support, at its current rates of use, a fivefold increase in urban population, and this without extracting a single new drop of water from streams and aquifers." Riebsame argues that 80–90 percent of western water is used for agriculture. He goes so far as to say "The West is too wet."[13] He adds, however, that getting that water won't be "painless." That's the understatement of the decade.

My reading of New Mexico's situation is much different than that. If Albuquerque doesn't get its annual forty-eight thousand acre-feet of San Juan/Chama Project water, John Stomp, city water planner, told me, the city will go south to Socorro and Sierra Counties and buy up all the water rights it can. In fact, farmers and organic growers in the south say Albuquerque is already looking for paper water. And if that isn't enough, the city can always go out to Grants, I hear, and buy water from its Blue Lake aquifer, the same water that Peabody Energy needs to use to run its expanded coal mine and proposed new power plant twenty-five miles north of Grants on the Lee Ranch. Everywhere I look, I see conflict when it comes to Albuquerque getting more water: conflict with Pueblos and their senior water rights, conflicts with the Navajo and their claims to San Juan Basin water, conflicts with acequia associations, with farmers, with other municipalities and developments, with river advocates and endangered species conservationists, and the venerable Middle Rio Grande Conservancy District and its hundreds of miles of irrigation and drainage canals in the Middle Rio Grande Valley. The MRGCD contends that any draining off of the agricultural water from its unlined ditch system will threaten the trees and green spaces in the North and South Valleys and fundamentally destroy their semi-rural character. There just seems no end to conflict, because New Mexico is not too wet.

And the weather isn't helping either. Scientists are reportedly worrying about the last three dry years here being the beginning of a ten- to twenty-year drought. The last one of those, in the mid 1950s, saw Elephant Butte Lake go dry as a bone for almost three years. Albuquerque's aquifer, the USGS tells us, is being depleted so fast that we could be in a crisis situation within forty years even with new San Juan/Chama water. The arithmetic just never quite adds up when highly touted city conservation efforts are compared to growth projections.

Horror stories in other towns abound around us, too. Santa Fe has been on stringent water restrictions for the last two years. Las Vegas, New Mexico, has had year-round water conservation measures in effect since 1999. They're both just plain running out of water. Las Vegas has been using too much of the flow from its main water source, the Gallinas River, and is being sued by acequia farmers downstream. And even with that extra water, Las Vegas still can't bring its water budget into the black. El Paso and Juarez are years, not decades, away from outgrowing their rights to underground water, and Alamagordo is so hard up it's thinking about desalinization and using heavily treated waste water for drinking. Mexico has its own claims to Rio Grande and Pecos river water that might impinge on farming practices on the east side of the state.

Questions about water quality still rise up from time to time, as well, even though nobody really wants to think about them. Even boomer optimism can't avoid superfund sites in the South Valley and West Mesa, EPA warnings about high arsenic levels in our water, controversies over an old nuclear waste dump on Sandia Base, endless news reports of leaking underground gasoline storage tanks and septic systems in the Valleys, not to mention hundreds of anecdotal stories over the years of increased birth defects and other maladies in the South Valley around the convergence of an old meat-packing plant, above-ground petroleum storage tanks, and numerous defense contractors and the plume of contaminants that state and federal scientists have been tracking for years.

Water is not something you can bank on in New Mexico. As an editorial in the *Santa Fe New Mexican* put it, "This is a desert state of over-diverted rivers, over-pumped aquifers and over-subscribed water rights; we can't go on behaving as if we live on the Mississippi Delta."[14] For all the transportation and land-use plans Albuquerque and New Mexico have generated over the years, it's an amazement to me that we still have nothing that resembles a regional water use plan, much less a state water use plan. We don't even have an accurate, or at least credible, inventory of all our water sources that the public and their representatives could readily refer to.

In all the thousands of news reports about water in the last years, I have never seen a reliable, hard-number estimate on how much pumpable water Albuquerque has left in its aquifer. I'm sure an exact number is hard to get. But not to have even a ballpark figure in public circulation makes the rest of the calculations virtually meaningless. If we don't know how much we have, how can we subtract our yearly usage from the total and project how much time we have until it's all gone? Yet we keep building golf courses. If we don't link population growth to water usage soon, then all our conservation measures and projections are pure fantasy, based on our current metro-area population of 727,000. The Middle Rio Grande Council of Governments forecasts our population will double by 2050. A mere twenty years from now, we'll have grown to 950,000. If 60 percent of city water use is residential, such a population explosion will make conservation meaningless. And even if we do secure the 48,000 acre-feet a year from the San Juan/ Chama Project, how's that going to help us fifty years from now when our children are ready to retire, if we've added, say, another 100,000 acre-feet of residential usage to our current 170,000 acre-feet a year pumped from the aquifer?

Add to all this the rise of the Pueblos as major players in development around Albuquerque's fringes, including the possibility of ninety-nine-year lease subdivisions, and the water issues all up and down the Middle Rio Grande Valley become a consternating mess of uncertainties. There's no question that Pueblo developers will become the target of others who complain about their so-called special privileges as "sovereign" entities, and who bitterly argue against their senior claims to water, and their often legally and historically well-documented ownership of contested lands.

Most observers would agree, I think, that the best privately financed large developments in our region of late have come from the Pueblos. The Santa Ana casino/hotel complex outside of Bernalillo could have been an aesthetic disaster, but it's amazingly low key architecturally and aware of its place in the landscape. And Santa Ana's brand-new Hyatt Tamaya hotel, down by the pueblo's part of the bosque, is arguably among the handsomest, least obtrusive, most New Mexican of new hotels in the state. What a far cry Tamaya is from the anonymous but skyline-dominating Hyatt hotel towers in downtown Albuquerque, subsidized by federal grants, with city hall as the architect's client. Albuquerque's officials characteristically took what they could get, which was a clone of buildings in Texas. Santa Ana's officials demanded and got a building with the sense of place they wanted.

Once it accumulated sufficient capital, Sandia Pueblo abandoned its eyesore white tent casino on I-25, and created an elegant, low-lying, land-respecting casino on the lower foothills of the Sandias that is a model of how such developments should be designed. Far from being a disrespectful monstrosity that ruins the view of the mountains, Sandia's casino complex puts to shame the developers who have cluttered up the West and East Mesas with standard, anyplace strip malls, glaring signage, and subdivisions.

There's little doubt among architects and planners I know that Sandia, Isleta, and Santa Ana are planning more development, possibly subdivisions to compete with the more shoddy work of non-tribal developers. They could raise the standard considerably, while sucking up more and more water from the aquifer. Sandia Pueblo's Governor Stuwart Paisano plans to go slowly in working with the two thousand developable acres around his casino, where it's possible new restaurants, high-end retail outlets, and perhaps even housing could be built. "We're in a position where we don't have to act right away," Paisano was quoted as saying.[15] From what I've seen so far, if necessity demands, I'd welcome a development between westside developers and the Pueblos. I'd bet the Pueblos could build better-quality houses in perhaps even innovative clusters and enclaves, like La Luz, on the West Mesa, and use the marketplace to force other developers to clean up their acts.

It's the work Santa Ana and Sandia have done so far on their bosques that sets them apart in our region. Both tribes have been working to restore the bosque under their control, clearing out non-native plants, removing the fire hazards of old timber, and generally opening up the riverside woods to become, once again, a usable and spacious gallery of cottonwoods much like it was before the war. I think of that effort and compare it to how developers and politicians have allowed the westside to go to pot, a planning disaster that has left residents there with the worst roads in the metro area. What could be more of a disaster than the donkey trail known as Golf Course Road, which passes for a major north-south arterial on the westside? That's a road elected officials allowed developers to get away with, a haphazard, afterthought of a road that everyone has to use and hates, as they wait and wait in long lines cursing who knows who. How does something like that get built? By default. And who defaulted? The Albuquerque area leadership-elite.

The overall picture of the last ten years tells a sad story of lost promise, lost opportunity, and failed leadership that amounts to a metro-area that's grown in a state of anarchy—undisciplined, imprudent, unrestrained. And yet, despite all the overextension of resources, all the wasteful unlimited development and generic new design, all the heedlessness to warnings about water shortages, and the stubborn insistence on maintaining the unworkable status quo at any price, Albuquerque remains in places pretty much the inviting city it has always been, a college town, a scientific utopia, the intellectual center of America's most foreign state, a place of vast natural beauty and enormous human talent whose physical form is still happily overshadowed by the grandeur of its high desert landscape. But for how long?

When Albuquerque lost its triple-A Dodger farm team, The Albuquerque Dukes, which went to the northwest coast, city movers and shakers, including its bankers and investment moguls, couldn't put up the civic energy, or the bucks, to find on their own another baseball team, despite the efforts of Mayor Jim Baca and the overwhelming support of this sports-crazed community. The leadership elite was looking after its own business as usual, and not paying its civic dues. Mayor Baca finally found a Chicago financier, Mike Koldyke, who summers with his family outside of Las Vegas, New Mexico, to come to the city's rescue, buy another team, and stimulate the construction of a new stadium. This seemingly unrelated incident mirrors what seems to me to be the dominant mindset in Albuquerque since 1992—a leadership elite that works almost exclusively for private gain and does relatively nothing to influence constructive and realistic public policy. And I'm troubled that I see no political alternative in the works, certainly nothing approaching the kind of coalition building that has helped environmentalists and ranchers create a new spirit of cooperation and scientific give and take about how best to use private and public leased grazing land. Albuquerque needs the leadership of a powerful group of enlightened business leaders, smart-growth advocates, cultural activists, environmentalists, farmers, developers, and labor unions to do the kind of serious thinking and jawboning it takes to break through the status quo of city building by default. But I've yet to see anything like that on the political horizon.

It may well be that the only thing that can rescue Albuquerque's built environment from total generic anarchy over the next decade is the harsh discipline of necessity in the form of an international oil crisis, price hikes, drought, and the inevitable water wars and growing shortages that no one, not even boomer optimists, can explain away any longer as environmental hype and illusion. Albuquerque's years of internal struggle since World War II, its fundamental political war between advocates of prudent, regional, respectful growth and helter-skelter do-anything-anywhere sprawl, could well be decided in the next twenty years when limits are reached and local leadership has to take its civic duty seriously and start to do what it takes to make Albuquerque into a city that adapts itself to its natural surroundings and arid conditions, and begins the long process of learning how to design with nature and not against it.

The major challenge of designing with nature in the new millennium, it seems to me, is for all large cities in the West to begin the creative and political processes necessary to retrofit themselves to meet increasingly harsh conditions, or to simply survive extended interim periods in which old, worn-out forms of energy and energy-infrastructures are replaced by new technologies on a massive scale. And that time seems to be coming fast. Although New Mexico is about to put online seven new power generation plants, large and small, to export energy to Phoenix and Southern California, in hopes of avoiding the price gouging electric shortages of 2001, at some point the grid, along with major gasoline pipelines and sea lanes, might simply become too dangerous as a national security threat to be allowed to exist in their present condition.[16] Although the other major cities in the West are probably beyond retrofitting their urban form, reduced instead to gearing up new transportation strategies and techniques, Albuquerque still has something of a chance to design itself out of the disastrous consequences of a major energy shortfall. But the window of opportunity is shrinking in a hurry. The more Rio Rancho continues to support and even stimulate growth on its farthest boundaries, the more Los Lunas and Belen expand, the more Sandoval County becomes a corporate and industrial "bedroom community" for Albuquerque, then the more constricted our opportunities become and the more the Middle Rio Grande Valley approaches the point of no return in which we, too, will be reduced to enduring drastic economic downturns and painful life changes while American industry converts to new power sources. And like every other major car town in the West, new energy sources, however utopian, will do little to solve our common desperate problem—climate fluctuations, water shortages, a ruination of the ecological commons, and might-makes-right water laws across state and international boundaries. It seems that Albuquerque has really only one chance to compete successfully with other western cities, while it still can. It must learn how to prosper while prudently anticipating energy transitions and reducing its water consumption, something that no other mammoth urban competitor is equipped to do anymore. Perhaps Albuquerque's isolation and boomless economy will prove to be unintended blessings in a new world in which even just being a little smaller and more compact gives a city a competitive edge in surviving hard times. Although I think a trend analysis of Albuquerque politics since World War II makes such a hope objectively unfounded, I still believe it's better to court the energy of naive optimism than settle into the inertia of cynical depression.

Notes

PREFACE

1. Cartoonist J. P. Rini referred to New Mexico as a "promised land" in "Residence in Promised Lands," *Century*, 3 December 1980, p. 16. Rini was the magazine's cofounder and managing editor.

2. Albuquerque was named for Don Francisco Fernández de la Cueva Enríquez, Duke of Alburquerque, Viceroy of New Spain, 1702–1708. "It was he, Governor Cuervo y Valdez of New Mexico sought to flatter by gracing the new villa on the Rio Grande with his noble name," writes Marc Simmons in *Albuquerque: A Narrative History* (Albuquerque: University of New Mexico Press, 1982), p. 92.

INTRODUCTION: THE VALUE OF LOCALITY

1. Lester R. Brown and Jodi L. Jacobson, *The Future of Urbanization: Facing the Ecological and Economic Constraints*, Worldwatch Paper #77 (Washington, D.C.: Worldwatch Institute, 1987), p. 6.

2. *Ibid.*, p. 5.

3. *The 1991 World Almanac and Book of Facts* (New York: Pharos Books, 1991), p. 557.

4. Todd Gitlin, "Postmodernism Defined, At Last," *Dissent*, (Winter 1989), reprinted in the *Utne Reader*, (July–August 1989), p. 61.

5. David H. Morrissey, "Atomic Economy: The Defense Industry in New Mexico," *Albuquerque Journal*, 23 March 1986.

6. John Naisbitt, *Megatrends: Ten New Directions Transforming Our Lives* (New York: Warner Books, 1982), p. 250.

7. Jack E. Leaman, "Keep Albuquerque Special: Everybody Must Work Hard to Preserve City's Southwest Character," *Albuquerque Journal*, 21 March 1986 (Op. Ed. page).

8. John L. Kessell, ed., *Remote Beyond Compare, Letters From Don Diego de Vargas to His Family From New Spain and New Mexico, 1675–1706*, (Albuquerque: University of New Mexico Press, 1990).

1
TIME AND PLACE

1. Rina Swentzell, "The Butterfly Effect: A Conversation with Rina Swentzell," *El Palacio* (Fall-Winter 1989), p. 28.

2. "Whose Britain Is It?", *Newsweek*, 13 November 1989, p. 84.

3. This figure comes from a conversation with Southwest archaeologist David E. Stuart. Stephen Lekson, curator of archaeology at the Museum of New Mexico, points out that Phoenix also sits atop a vast network of ancient settlements, one of which is called Los Muertos. This reminder appears in his paper entitled "Anasazi Communities in Context," presented to the symposium on Anasazi Architecture and American Design, Mesa Verde National Park, May 1991.

4. Edward P. Dozier, *The Pueblo Indians of North America* (New York: Holt, Rinehart and Winston, 1970), pp. 4–5.

5. Marc Simmons, *Albuquerque: A Narrative History* (Albuquerque: University of New Mexico Press, 1982), p. 93.

6. *Ibid.*, p. 170.

7. Byron Johnson, curator of history, Albuquerque Museum, unpublished chronology of Albuquerque, p. 5.

8. *Ibid.*, p. 8.

9. Simmons, p. 362.

10. David H. Morrissey, "Atomic Economy: The Defense Industry in New Mexico," *Albuquerque Journal*, 23 March 1986.

11. Johnson, p. 101.

12. Simmons, p. 347.

13. Robert Fishman, "America's New City: Megapolis Unbound," *Wilson Quarterly* (Winter 1990), p. 25.

14. Tom Harmon, "Ditch Bank Chronicles: Shading Up," *Albuquerque Journal*, 11 July 1987.

15. Fishman, p. 30.

2

REPUTATION AND IDENTITY

1. *The 1989 Information Please Almanac*, (Boston: Houghten Mifflin, 1989) p. 767.

2. Lewis Mumford, *Sticks and Stones: A Study of American Architecture and Civilization* (New York: Dover, 1955), p. 21.

3. *Time*, 4 April 1988, p. 47.

4. Tom Wolfe, *The Right Stuff* (New York: Farrar, Straus & Giroux, 1979), p. 88.

5. "Albuquerque, Las Cruces Rate High in Stress," *Albuquerque Journal*, 14 October 1988.

6. Paul Weingarten, "Assignment: Albuquerque, Town Tries to Wash its Hands of Image of Mud Huts, Burros," *Chicago Tribune*, 5 May 1987 (Op. Ed. page).

7. Ellen Marks, "Ads to Battle View of City as Cow Town," *Albuquerque Journal*, 4 April 1987.

8. Bob Shacochis, "In Deepest Gringolandia, Mexico: The Third World as Tourist Theme Park," *Harper's Magazine*, July 1989, p. 42.

9. John Naisbitt, *Megatrends: Ten New Directions Transforming Our Lives* (New York: Warner Books, 1982), p. 250.

10. I'm referring here to heavily supported but failed efforts in the 1970s to create an international airport on the West Mesa and to bridge the Rio Grande at Montaño Road in the mid North Valley.

11. This is a term frequently used by cultural historian William Irwin Thompson in his book *Passages About Earth: An Exploration of the New Planetary Culture*, (New York: Harper & Row Publishers, 1973).

12. William Sharpe and Leonard Wallock, eds., *Visions of the Modern City*, (Baltimore: Johns Hopkins University Press, 1987), p. 29.

13. *Ibid.*, p. 31.

14. Lewis Mumford, *The City In History* (New York: Harcourt, Brace, & World, 1961), p. 33.

15. Antoine Predock, "Housing—Five Different Stories," *Mass: Journal of the School of Architecture and Planning, UNM* (Summer 1984), pp. 8–9.

16. Susan Dewitt, *Historic Albuquerque Today* (Albuquerque: City of Albuquerque, 1978), p. 118.

17. *Albuquerque Chapter, New Mexico Society of Architects Newsletter* (July 1989), p. 5.

18. David Dillon, "Cities Sprawling in the Desert: Albuquerque," *Architecture*, March 1984, p. 138.

19. Edna E. Heatherington, "Albuquerque's Unique Airport will Retain its Regional Style After the Expansion," *New Mexico Architecture*, March–April 1988, p. 25.

20. Architectural historian Chris Wilson of Albuquerque made this observation during a conversation with me in 1990, in the airport coffee shop.

21. Urban critic William H. Whyte used this phrase in describing the Albuquerque Convention Center in a piece by Charles Moore, "City's Public Spaces Get Low Marks From Designer," *Albuquerque Journal*, 25 April 1986.

22. Robert Venturi, *Complexity and Contradiction in Architecture* (New York: Museum of Modern Art, 1966), pp. 22–23.

23. Robert Venturi, Denise Scott Brown, and Steven Izenour, *Learning from Las Vegas* (Cambridge: M.I.T. Press, 1977), p. 3.

24. Peter Blake, "Vulgarian Chic," *Interior Design*, July 1986, p. 262.

3

ALBUQUERQUE AND SANTA FE

1. James Clifford, *The Predicament of Culture* (Cambridge: Harvard University Press, 1988), p. 15.

2. *Ibid.*, p. 14.

3. Barry Schlachter, "Trendy Capital Sports Fake Adobe and Eurotrash," *Albuquerque Journal*, 2 October 1989.

4. Sally Ann Stewart, *Santa Fe a Divided Boomtown, USA Today*, 6 March 1990.

5. *Ibid.*

6. Shlachter.

7. Beverley Spears, "The Westside Guadalupe Historic District: Hispanic Vernacular v. Pueblo Revival," a paper presented at the symposium on Pueblo Style and Regional Architecture, University of New Mexico, Albuquerque, 1988.

8. Jim Danneskiold, "Survey Finds Anti-Growth Sentiment in Santa Fe," *Albuquerque Journal*, 22 February 1990.

9. Jim Danneskiold, "Santa Fe Losing Its Charm for Residents Poll Shows," *Albuquerque Journal*, 21 February 1989.

10. Nicholas C. Markovich, Wolfgang F. E. Preiser, and Fred G. Sturm, eds., *Pueblo Style and Regional Architecture* (New York: Van Nostrand Reinhold, 1990), p. viii.

11. "Santa Fe: The City in Print," *Century*, 21 April 1982, p. 6.

12. Winfield Townley Scott, *Exiles and Fabrications* (New York: Doubleday, 1961), pp. 213–14.

13. Ian Nairn, *The American Landscape* (New York: Random House, 1965), pp. 5–6.

14. Jack Ehn, "The City Similar" *Albuquerque Tribune*, 23 February 1990.

15. Chris Wilson, "The Myth of Santa Fe: Anglo, Pueblo, and Hispanic Uses of an Invented Regional Tradition," paper presented at the Society of Architectural Historians, Boston, February 1990, p. 2.

16. *Ibid.*

17. Markovich, Preiser, and Sturm, pp. 198–205.

18. Chris Wilson, "The Milagro Bean Field War and the Paradox of Cultural Identity," unpublished essay.

19. Marc Simmons, *Albuquerque: A Narrative History* (Albuquerque: University of New Mexico Press, 1982), p. 317.

20. "Conversations In Santa Fe With Lewis Mumford," *New Mexico Architect*, January-February 1963, p. 5.

21. *Ibid.*, p. 6.

22. *Ibid.*, pp. 6–7.

23. Wilhelm Kücker, "Architecture as Backdrop," *Kultur Chronik: News and Views from the Federal Republic of Germany*, No. 3 (1988), pp. 31–33.

24. *Ibid.*, p. 31.

25. *Ibid.*, p. 32.

26. Susan Dewitt, *Historic Albuquerque Today* (Albuquerque: City of Albuquerque, 1978), p. 28.

4

MODERNISM AND REGIONALISM

1. Edna Heatherington Bergman, *The Fate of Architectural Theory in Albuquerque, New Mexico: Buildings of Four Decades, 1920–1960* (Master of Architecture Thesis, University of New Mexico, 1978), p. 301.

2. Chris Wilson, "Regionalism Redefined: The Impact of Modernism in New Mexico," *Mass: Journal of the School of Architecture and Planning, UNM* (Spring 1983), p. 16.

3. Conversation with Rina Swentzell at Mesa Verde, Fall, 1987.

4. V. B. Price, "The Pueblo University," *New Mexico Magazine*, September 1978, p. 18.

5. *Ibid.*

6. Architectural historian Chris Wilson feels it is "not unreasonable" to assume that Tight and Cristy were both familiar with the Pueblo Indian room at the Alvarado Hotel, a Fred Harvey enterprise which opened in Albuquerque in 1902.

7. Carleen Lazzell, "Early Spanish–Pueblo Revival Architecture at the University of New Mexico," *New Mexico Historical Review* (January 1989), p. 23.

8. Wilson, p. 17.

9. V. B. Price, "The Pueblo University," *New Mexico Magazine*, September 1978, p. 18.

10. George Clayton Pearl, "In Memoriam: John Gaw Meem 1892–1983," *Mass: Journal of the School of Architecture and Planning, UNM* (Summer 1984), p. 30.

11. John Gaw Meem, "Old Forms for New Buildings," *Mass: Journal of the School of Architecture and Planning, University of New Mexico* (Spring 1983), p. 8.

12. Bergman, p. 302.

13. *Ibid.*, p. 304.

14. Wilson, p. 17.

15. George Clayton Pearl, "Buildings of Context: Van Dorn Hooker at UNM," *Century*, 1 October 1980, p. 18.

5

A CITY OF OPEN SPACES

1. Ian McHarge, *Design With Nature* (New York: Doubleday, 1969), p. 154.

2. Baker H. Morrow, *A Dictionary of Landscape Architecture* (Albuquerque: University of New Mexico Press, 1987), p. 225.

3. *Annual Report, City of Albuquerque Open Space Advisory Board*, 1 July 1988 to 30 June 1989, from the unpaginated "Introduction and Purpose of Report."

4. Daniel Pedersen, "A Delicate Balance on the Land," *Newsweek*, 6 February 1989, p. 49.

5. *Annual Report*, p. 3.

6. Byron Johnson, curator of history, Albuquerque Museum, unpublished chronology of Albuquerque, p. 136.

7. *Ibid.*, p. 134.

8. Tom Turner, "Who Speaks for the Future," *Sierra*, published by the Sierra Club, July-August 1990, pp. 30–38, 67–72.

9. Johnson, p. 134.

10. Gregory Bateson, *Mind and Nature* (New York: Bantam Books, 1980), p. 7.

11. Patricia O'Connor, "Albuquerque Musings: Wilson Hurley, Artist," *New Mexico Progress*, published by SunWest Financial Services, Albuquerque, May 1990.

12. Marc Simmons, *Albuquerque: A Narrative History* (Albuquerque, University of New Mexico Press, 1982), p. 97.

13. Karen McPhearson, "Rock Art Park Faces Rocky Start," *Albuquerque Tribune*, 29 June 1990.

14. *Ibid.*

15. From the proceedings of "Open Space Connections," the 1987 National Open Space Conference in Albuquerque, October 1987, p. 97.

16. McHarge, p. 197.

17. McPhearson.

18. *Ibid.*

19. J. B. Jackson, *Discovering the Vernacular Landscape* (New Haven: Yale University Press, 1984), p. 40.

20. Edward Relph, *The Modern Urban Landscape* (Baltimore: Johns Hopkins University Press, 1987), pp. 253–54.

6

A SPIRITUAL REGION

1. Vincent Scully, *Pueblo: Mountain, Village, Dance* (New York: Viking Press, 1975), p. 9.

2. The concept of a pan-Pueblo cosmology appears in archaeologist Michael P. Marshall's foreword, "The Ancient Cosmography of Chaco Canyon," in *Chaco Body* by photographer Kirk Gittings and poet V. B. Price (Albuquerque: Artspace Press, 1991).

3. Rina Swentzell, "An Understated Sacredness," *Mass: Journal of the School of Architecture and Planning, UNM* (Fall 1985), pp. 24–25.

4. Alfonso Ortiz, *The Tewa World: Space, Time, Being and Becoming in a Pueblo Society* (Chicago: University of Chicago Press, 1969) p. 19.

5. Scully, p. 1.

6. Tony Anella, "Learning from the Pueblos," in *Pueblo Style and Regional Architecture*, edited by Nicholas C. Markovich, Wolfgang E. Poerses, and Fred Sturm (New York: Van Nostrand Reinhold, 1990), p. 36.

7. Susan Dewitt, *Historic Albuquerque Today* (Albuquerque: Albuquerque City Government, 1978), p. 50.

7

A CITY OF BABEL

1. "What Became of the Public Square," *Harper's Magazine*, July 1990, p. 49.

2. Roberta Brandes Gratz, *The Living City* (New York: Simon & Schuster, 1989), p. 385.

3. *La Confluencia* was a multicultural periodical published in Albuquerque in the mid 1970s, edited by Susan Dewitt and Pat D'Andrea. Prophetic of the 1990s, the magazine focused on New Mexico as a confluence of cultures.

4. "Duke City May be Hazardous to Home Life, Magazine Says," *Albuquerque Journal*, 16 April 1987.

5. *Ibid*.

6. Rick Boyer, *Places Rated Almanac: Your Guide to Finding the Best Places to Live in America*, 2d ed. (Chicago: Rand McNally, 1985), p. 448.

7. Herb Smith, former Albuquerque city manager, quotes this unnamed planning commissioner in his book *Planning America's Communities: Paradise Found? Paradise Lost?* (Chicago: Planners Press, American Planning Association, 1991), p. 168.

8. Howard Rabinowitz, "Albuquerque: City at a Crossroads," in *Sunbelt Cities: Politics and Growth Since World War II*, ed. Richard M. Bernard and Bradley R. Rice (Austin: University of Texas Press, 1983), p. 257.

9. Rene Kimball, "City Zeroes in On Services for the Needy," *Albuquerque Journal*, 16 April 1987.

10. *Southwest Area Plan*, City of Albuquerque, undated, vol. IV, "The Plan," p. ii.

11. Edward Relph, *The Modern Urban Landscape* (Baltimore: Johns Hopkins University Press, 1987), p. 140.

12. V. B. Price, " 'Hicks' Deserve Courtesy, Too," *Albuquerque Tribune*, 8 December 1989.

13. V. B. Price, "Flooding in Both Valleys Has Become a Public Scandal," *Albuquerque Tribune*, 27 July 1990.

8

A CITY AT THE END OF THE WORLD

1. Marc Simmons, "Misery as a Factor in New Mexican Colonial Life," in *Reflections: Papers on Southwestern Culture History in Honor of Charles H. Lange*, Papers of the Archaeological Society of New Mexico no. 14 (Santa Fe: Ancient City Press, 1988), pp. 227–28.

2. John L. Kessell, ed., *Remote Beyond Compare, Letters From Don Diego de Vargas to His Family from New Spain and New Mexico, 1675–1706* (Albuquerque: University of New Mexico Press, 1990).

3. *1991 World Almanac and Book of Facts* (New York: Pharos Books, 1991), p. 552.

4. Ian Nairn, *The American Landscape: A Critical View* (New York: Random House, 1965), p. 5.

5. Gro Harlem Brundtland, *Our Common Future: World Commission on Environment and Development* (Oxford: Oxford University Press, 1987), pp. 43–45.

6. Kevin Lynch, *Good City Form* (Cambridge: M.I.T. Press, 1981), p. 251.

7. Rina Swentzell, "The Butterfly Effect: A Conversation with Rina Swentzell," *El Palacio* (Fall/Winter 1989), p. 28.

8. Kevin Roderick, "Living in Los Angeles Losing its Luster," *Albuquerque Journal*, 22 February 1989.

9. E. A. Torriero, "Once-Utopian Los Angeles Verging on Urban Disaster," *Albuquerque Journal*, 30 July 1989.

10. Ellen Uzelac, "Thousands Flee Crime, Smog in Once-Utopian L. A.," *Albuquerque Journal*, 28 August 1989.

11. Lewis Mumford, *The City in History* (New York: Harcourt, Brace & World, 1961), p. 109.

12. Robert Fishman, "America's New City: Megapolis Unbound," *Wilson Quarterly* (Winter 1990), p. 25.

13. Susan Lewis, "Cartel Envisions Developed West Side," *Albuquerque Tribune*, 30 April 1987.

14. Tony Davis, "Albuquerque Water Supply May Have Limit," *Albuquerque Tribune*, 20 February 1989.

15. "Ground-Water Protection Policy and Action Plan," Citizen Summary 3 and 4, Albuquerque/Bernalillo County Environmental Health Departments, May/June 1990.

16. Wendell Berry, "The Politics of Home," *Utne Reader*, May/June 1990, p. 84.

9

PROMISES, PROMISES

1. The infamous map was attached to an article by Ross E. Millay called "Anthrax Hides Along Cattle Trails of the Old West." It appeared in the *New York Times,* October 29, 2001 on page A9.

2. V. B. Price, *A City at the End of the World* (Albuquerque: University of New Mexico Press, 1992), p. 138.

3. Longtime local observer Wally Gordon made this assessment in his article "Analysis" Edgewood Makes History," in an East Mountain tabloid called *The Independent,* which has nothing to do with the venerable, but defunct, *New Mexico Independent* run for years in the 1970s and 1980s by Mark and Mary Beth Acuff. See *The Independent,* December 5–11, 2001, p. 13.

4. This remarkable document was published on September 8, 1986 and covered everything from population growth, healthcare, crime, and the economy to the water supply, education, transportation, and the environment.

5. *Nuestro Pueblo,* fall 2001, p. 3. A copy can be obtained from 1000 Friends of New Mexico.

6. Kate Nash, "Group takes pre-emptive strike at Paseo extension," the *Albuquerque Tribune,* mid-November, 2001, p. A1.

7. The *Albuquerque Journal,* November 23, 2001, editorial page.

8. The Planned Growth Strategy is billed as being "NOT 'no growth' or 'slow growth'," presumably in an effort to detach the idea of growth management from the bogus accusation that conservationists advocate no growth. The two volumes of The Planned Growth Strategy have no date or other references attached to them. I remember receiving my copies some time in early to mid-2001. The city council and county commission will consider it, observers assumed, before the end of 2002.

9. These are spelled out in an undated, unauthored handout that accompanied the two-volume Strategy.

10. The Planned Growth Strategy, volume two, p. 4–11.

11. "Just The Beginning," ABQBiz, the weekly business section of the *Albuquerque Tribune,* January 21, 2002, p.1.

12.

13. William E. Riebsame, "Geographies of the New West," in *Across the Great Divide: Exploration in Collaborative Conservation and the American West,* edited by Philip Brick, Donald Snow, and Sarah Van de Wetering (Washington, D.C.: Island Press, 2001), p. 50.

14. *Santa Fe New Mexican,* January 19, 2002, p. A-5.

15. Patrick Armijo, "Tribe's Plan Is Cautious," *Albuquerque Journal,* Westside, November 24, 2001, p. A-1.

16. Amory B. Lovins and L. Hunter Lovins, "Energy Forever," *The American Prospect,* February 11, 2002, pp. 30–34.

Selected Bibliography

Albuquerque/Bernalillo County Comprehensive Plan. Albuquerque: Planning Department, City of Albuquerque, 1987.

Albuquerque/Bernalillo County Comprehensive Historic Preservation Plan. Albuquerque: Planning Department, Redevelopment Division, City of Albuquerque, undated.

An Introduction to the Study of the Future. Washington, D.C.: World Future Society, 1977.

Annual Report: City of Albuquerque Open Space Advisory Board. Albuquerque: Open Space Division, City of Albuquerque, 1989.

Banham, Reyner. *Los Angeles: The Architecture of Four Ecologies.* Baltimore: Pelican Books, 1973.

Barth, Gunther. *Instant Cities: Urbanization and the Rise of San Francisco and Denver.* Albuquerque: University of New Mexico Press, 1988.

Bateson, Gregory. *Mind and Nature.* New York: Bantam Books, 1980.

Bernard, Richard M., and Bradley R. Rice, eds. *Sunbelt Cities: Politics and Growth Since World War II.* Austin: University of Texas Press, 1983.

Biebel, Charles D. *Making the Most of It: Public Works in Albuquerque During the Great Depression 1929–1942.* Albuquerque: Albuquerque Museum, 1986.

Brown, Lester R., and Jodi L. Jacobson. *The Future of Urbanization: Facing the Ecological and Economic Constraints*, World Watch Paper #77. Washington, D.C.: World Watch Institute, 1987.

Brundtland, Gro Harlem. *Our Common Future: World Commission on Environment and Development*. Oxford: Oxford University Press, 1987.

Bunting, Bainbridge. *Early Churches in New Mexico*. Albuquerque: University of New Mexico Press, 1976.

——. *John Gaw Meem: Southwestern Architect*. Albuquerque: University of New Mexico Press, 1983.

Clifford, James. *The Predicament of Culture*. Cambridge: Harvard University Press, 1988.

Dewitt, Susan. *Historic Albuquerque Today*. Albuquerque: City of Albuquerque, 1978.

Downtown Core Revitalization Strategy. Albuquerque: Planning Department, Redevelopment Division, City of Albuquerque, 1989.

Dozier, Edward P. *The Pueblo Indians of North America*. New York: Holt, Rinehart and Winston, 1970.

Eberle, Jay A. *Preliminary Background Report for the Planning and Management of Archaeological Resources in Albuquerque/Bernalillo County*. Albuquerque: Community and Economic Development Department, City of Albuquerque, 1984.

Farbstein, Jay, and Min Kantrowitz. *People in Places: Experiencing, Using, and Changing the Built Environment*. Englewood Cliffs: Prentice-Hall, Inc., 1978.

Fergusson, Harvey. *Home in the West*. New York: Duell, Sloan and Pearce, 1944.

Goals for Albuquerque, 1983–84. Albuquerque: City of Albuquerque, 1984.

Gratz, Roberta Brandes. *The Living City*. New York: Simon & Schuster, 1989.

Hall, Edward T. *The Hidden Dimension*. Garden City: Doubleday Anchor Books, 1969.

Holland, Laurence B., ed. *Who Designs America?* Garden City: Doubleday Anchor Books, 1966.

Jackson, J. B. *Discovering the Vernacular Landscape.* New Haven: Yale University Press, 1984.

Jacobs, Jane. *The Death and Life of Great American Cities.* New York: Vintage Books, 1961.

——. *The Economy of Cities.* New York: Vintage Books, 1970.

Kelley, Vincent C. *Albuquerque: Its Mountains, Valley, Water, and Volcanoes.* Socorro: State Bureau of Mines and Mineral Resources, New Mexico Institute of Mining and Technology, 1969.

——. *Geology of the Albuquerque Basin.* Socorro: New Mexico Bureau of Mineral Resources, New Mexico Institute of Mining and Technology, 1977.

Kessell, John L., ed. *Remote Beyond Compare. Letters from Don Diego de Vargas to His Family from New Spain and New Mexico.* Albuquerque: University of New Mexico Press, 1989.

Kubler, George. *Religious Architecture of New Mexico.* 1940. Reissued Albuquerque: University of New Mexico Press, 1990.

Lynch, Kevin. *Good City Form.* Cambridge, Mass.: M.I.T. Press, 1981.

Markovich, Nicholas, Wolfgang F. E. Preiser, and Fred G. Sturm, eds. *Pueblo Style and Regional Architecture.* New York: Van Nostrand Reinhold, 1990.

McHarge, Ian. *Design with Nature.* New York: Doubleday, 1969.

Mumford, Lewis. *The City In History.* New York: Harcourt, Brace, & World, 1961.

——. *Sticks and Stones: A Study of American Architecture and Civilization.* New York: Dover, 1955.

Morrow, Baker H. *A Dictionary of Landscape Architecture.* Albuquerque: University of New Mexico Press, 1987.

Nairn, Ian. *The American Landscape.* New York: Random House, 1965.

Naisbitt, John. *Megatrends: Ten Directions Transforming Our Lives.* New York: Warner Books, 1982.

Nash, Gerald D. *The American West in the Twentieth Century: A Short History of an Urban Oasis.* Albuquerque: University of New Mexico Press, 1977.

Open Space Connections, proceedings of the 1989 National Open Space Conference in Albuquerque. Albuquerque: Albuquerque Conservation Trust, 1989.

Ortiz, Alfonso, ed. *Handbook of North American Indians: Southwest, Vol. 9.* Washington, D.C.: Smithsonian Institution, 1979.

———. *The Tewa World: Space, Time, and Becoming in a Pueblo Society.* Chicago: University of Chicago Press, 1969.

Relph, Edward. *The Modern Urban Landscape.* Baltimore: Johns Hopkins University Press, 1987.

Rosner, Hy and Joan Rosner. *Albuquerque's Environmental Story.* Albuquerque: Albuquerque Public School and the City of Albuquerque, 1985.

Sargeant, Kathryn and Mary Davis. *Shining River, Precious Land: An Oral History of Albuquerque's North Valley.* Albuquerque: Albuquerque Museum, 1986.

Scott, Winfield Townley. *Exiles and Fabrications.* New York: Doubleday, 1961.

Scully, Vincent. *Pueblo: Mountain, Village, Dance.* New York: Viking Press, 1975.

Sharpe, William and Leonard Wallock, eds. *Visions of the Modern City.* Baltimore: Johns Hopkins University Press, 1987.

Simmons, Marc. *Albuquerque: A Narrative History.* Albuquerque: University of New Mexico Press, 1982.

Smith, Herbert H. *Planning America's Communities: Paradise Found? Paradise Lost?* Chicago: Planners Press, 1991.

Spears, Beverley. *American Adobes: Rural Houses of Northern New Mexico.* Albuquerque: University of New Mexico Press, 1986.

Stern, Robert A. M., ed. *The Anglo-American Suburb.* London: Architectural Design, 1981.

———. *Pride of Place: Building the American Dream.* Boston: Houghton Mifflin, 1986.

Southwest Area Plan: Vol. IV, The Plan. Albuquerque: Planning Department, City of Albuquerque, undated.

Thompson, William Irwin. *Passages About Earth: An Exploration of the New Planetary Culture.* New York: Harper & Row, 1973.

Toffler, Alvin. *Future Shock.* New York: Bantam Books, 1970.

Venturi, Robert. *Complexity and Contradiction in Architecture.* New York: Museum of Modern Art, 1966.

Venturi, Robert, Denise Scott Brown, and Steven Isenour. *Learning From Las Vegas.* Cambridge, Mass.: M.I.T. Press, 1977.

Wagar, Warren. *The City of Man.* Baltimore: Penguin Books, 1967.

Weaver, John D. *Los Angeles: The Enormous Village, 1781–1981.* Santa Barbara: Capra Press, 1980.

Williams, Jerry L. *New Mexico in Maps.* Albuquerque: University of New Mexico Press, 1986.

Wolfe, Tom. *The Right Stuff.* New York: Farrar, Straus & Giroux, 1979.

Index